Honey Recipes

From a Welsh Kitchen

By Jane Jones

Honey Recipes
From a Welsh Kitchen

By Jane Jones

Jointly published by: The International Bee Research Association, a Company Limited by Guarantee, 1, Agincourt Street, Monmouth, NP25 3DZ (UK) & Northern Bee Books, Scout Bottom Farm, Mytholmroyd, Hebden Bridge HX7 5JS (UK).

Obtainable from:

www.ibra.org.uk & www.northernbeebooks.co.uk

Designed by: Joanne Hawker

ISBN: 978-1-913811-18-1

I B R A

INTERNATIONAL BEE
RESEARCH ASSOCIATION

The majority of the profits from the book go to the International Bee Research Association which is a registered charity devoted to spreading information on bees and thereby helping to save, protect and promote these much needed and currently threatened creatures.
Bees are the very key to our own food supply not through honey but through the pollination of fruit and vegetable crops essential to our varied diet.

The International Bee Research Association, Reg. Charity No: 209222

Honey Recipes

From a Welsh Kitchen

Content:

By Jane Jones

Forward

What goes around comes around. Today "recycling" and "sustainability" are words we hear every day as we are rightly urged to care for our fragile planet. For me, growing up in a remote forester's house, on the edge of the Brecon Beacons in the immediate post war years, re-cycling was something we did automatically. Remoteness and the austerity of the times also meant that sustainability came naturally as we had to have a certain amount of self-sufficiency with goats, chickens and bees housed at the end of the garden. It was a time of rationing and honey was, as it had been before the transportation of sugar from New World plantations, the main source of sweetness in our food and cooking.

Memories of those now distant days have been in part responsible for this book. My earlier publication – Traditional Welsh Honey Recipes – made me realise how much can be done with honey and so I have welcomed the opportunity, offered by the International Bee Research Association (IBRA), to expand and vary those recipes. All the contents have been tried and tested, on and by my own family and friends, who sometimes managed to eat the food before it could be photographed for the book which is, I suppose in its own way, a kind of recommendation! I hope that you, too, will enjoy, not only the end product, but also the making of these recipes which may well stimulate memories as well as appetites.

Preparing the food has been a joy, preparing the book has been hard work. Tony Gruba and Stuart Williams willingly took on the task of making many of the recipes thus helping me ensure that the instructions, as well as the ingredients, were understandable to a new reader. It was good to know that they had satisfaction from the cooking process as well as the food. I thank them for their help.

The book would not have been completed without the tireless support, the constructive criticism and suggestions of my daughter, Sarah Jones. She has been a formidable taskmaster and editor but I thank her for the precision I believe she has brought to my simple home cooking approach. My thanks also to Joanne Hawker for her creative design and layout, which I hope you will find helps when you use the book.

Enjoy these honey recipes from a Welsh kitchen.

Jane Jones
March 2011
Cardiff

1

Useful Tips For Cooking With Honey

Types of honey
All the honey used in this book is runny multifloral honey unless stated otherwise.

Delicate flavours can be lost in cooking so it is sometimes best to use some of the blended honeys which are widely available.

As a general rule, light honeys are used for sponge cakes, biscuits and desserts and darker ones for meat dishes, fruit cakes or recipes with chocolate.

Honey acts as a preservative, so it is very good for keeping cakes and biscuits fresh and moist.

Storage
Store honey in a dry place at room temperature. Refrigeration will speed up crystallization.

Sugar substitute
Honey can be used in most recipes instead of sugar, but as it is much sweeter there are a few points to remember:-
*   Start by substituting honey for up to one half of the sugar. With experimentation honey can be substituted for all the sugar in some recipes.
*   It is best for texture as well as flavour to retain some sugar.
*   The amount of liquid in a recipe should be reduced by a quarter, and in cakes half a teaspoon of baking soda added for every four tablespoons of honey.
*   Baked foods containing honey brown more quickly, therefore, the temperature should be reduced by 4°C to prevent over browning and flavour change.
*   All the recipes in this book have been adjusted accordingly.

Measuring honey
The easiest way to measure honey is by the tablespoon and to do this first dip the spoon in very hot water or coat in oil. This way you will find that the honey just slides off the spoon giving you an accurate measurement and no mess.

Some of the recipes in this book are in either ounces or tablespoons. As a general rule 1 oz = 1 tbsp.

Meat Recipes

From a Welsh Kitchen

Spicy Beef Medallions With Sesame Honey

Serves 4

200 ml Soy sauce	1 dsp Sesame seeds
50 ml Sesame oil	8 x 100 g - 3½ oz Beef medallions
4 Garlic cloves, crushed	3 - 4 tbsp Olive oil
¼ tsp Dried chilli flakes	8 Spring onions, with ends trimmed
3 tbsp Honey	

1. Put the soy sauce, sesame oil, garlic, chilli and honey into a saucepan over a moderate heat and simmer for 5 minutes. Remove from the heat and stir in the sesame seeds. Marinate the beef in some of the sauce for an hour.

2. Remove from the marinade. Heat 2 - 3 tsp of olive oil in a frying pan to smoking point, then fry the medallions for 3 minutes on each side.

3. Remove from the heat and rest. Heat 1 tbsp of olive oil in another pan and fry the spring onions until light brown.

4. Reheat the remaining sauce. Place the medallions on a plate and pour over the sauce. Garnish each piece of beef with the spring onions.

5. Serve with some homemade chips or potato wedges and a side salad.

Soy Honey Chicken With Sesame Spinach

The combination of honey, soy sauce, garlic and chilli turn a simple chicken breast into a romantic meal. The sesame spinach is a quick and easy side dish with a light oriental touch.

Serves 2

2 Large Chicken breasts, with skins	2 tbsp Soy sauce
1 Garlic clove	1 tbsp Honey
1 Small red chilli, finely sliced	1 tbsp Lime or lemon juice
1 tbsp Root ginger, finely chopped	1 tbsp Olive oil

For the Sauce:
1 tbsp Lime or Lemon juice   2 tbsp Thai chilli sauce

1. Preheat the oven to 200°C, gas mark 6.
Line a baking tray with foil.

2. Crush the garlic, half, and mix with the chilli and the ginger to make a paste. Add the soy sauce, honey, lime juice and olive oil. Stir well and leave to marinate for a few hours or over night.

3. Place the chicken breasts on the baking tray with the marinade, bake for 25 - 30 minutes basting once or twice. Cook until the skin is crispy and the chicken is cooked through. Rest for a few minutes while making the sauce.

4. Mix the Thai chilli sauce and lime juice and spoon around the chicken and spinach.

For the Sesame Spinach:

250 g - 9 oz Spinach	1 tbsp Butter
1 tbsp Sesame oil	Pepper and salt
	1 tsp Sesame seeds

1. Wash the spinach and place in a sauce pan with just enough water to cover the leaves. Cook for one minute, drain the wilted leaves and set aside. When cool squeeze them dry.

2. To serve reheat the spinach in a saucepan with the sesame oil, butter, pepper and salt, toss well and arrange on the plates with the chicken. Sprinkle the sesame seeds over the dish.

Welsh Lamb With Orange And Honey

Serves 4

1.3 kg - 3 lb Leg of lamb	3 Onions, peeled and quartered
Olive oil to rub over the meat	5 Garlic cloves
Pepper and salt to taste	2 - 3 Sprigs of thyme

For the Topping:	1 tbsp Sherry vinegar
150 ml - ¼ Pint of mead	1 Orange, the zest cut into fine strips
2 tbsp Honey	125 ml Orange juice

1. Preheat the oven to 220°C, gas mark 7.

2. Place the onions in a roasting tin and add the garlic and sprigs of thyme, then place the lamb on top. Rub the meat with the oil and sprinkle with salt and pepper. Roast for 20 minutes, basting regularly.

3. Reduce the temperature to 180°C, gas mark 4 and continue cooking for 2 hours.

4. To make the topping. Heat the mead in a small pan, add the sherry vinegar, orange juice and honey. Cook on a high heat for a few minutes until syrupy and then add the orange zest.

5. Remove the lamb from the oven and increase the temperature to a 200°C, gas mark 4. Pour the sauce over the meat, return to the oven for 10 minutes to absorb the sauce. Remove from the oven and leave to rest for at least 15 minutes before carving.

6. Serve with new potatoes and seasonal vegetables.

Sausages With Mustard And Honey

Serves 4

8 Large pork sausages : 3 heaped tbsp Runny honey
2 tbsp Grainy mustard : 2 tbsp Lemon juice
1 tbsp Smooth Dijon mustard :

1. Preheat the oven to 200°C, gas mark 6.

2. Put the sausages in a large roasting dish so that there is space between them. In a bowl mix the mustards, honey and lemon juice. Stir well and pour over the sausages.

3. Bake for 25 - 30 minutes. Occasionally rolling the sausages over in the mixture so that they are well coated and become sticky and glossy.

4. Serve with mashed potatoes or for an alternative try equal quantities of carrot and sweet potato boiled and mashed together. Arrange the sausages on top with a spoonful of the sticky sauce poured over them.

Chicken With Ginger And Honey

Serves 4

4 Chicken breasts : 2 tbsp Chopped ginger
3 tbsp Honey : 1 Garlic clove, crushed
1 tsp Olive oil, or a flavoured oil e.g. sesame : 1 tbsp Chopped oregano
1 tbsp Soy sauce :

1. Preheat the oven to 200°C, gas mark 6. Grease a large baking tray.

2. Mix together the honey, oil, soy sauce, ginger and garlic in a small saucepan over a low heat, stir well for a few minutes to combine.

3. Place the chicken breasts in an oven proof dish and pour over the marinade, coating each piece well. Cover with cling film and refrigerate for an hour.

4. Remove the chicken from the marinade. Place on the baking tray and cook in the oven for 15 minutes or until cooked through.

5. To serve sprinkle with the oregano and serve with vegetables or a green salad.

Pork Spare Ribs With Honey And Garlic

Serves 4

1 kg - 2½ lb Lean pork spare ribs	1 tsp Ground ginger
200 g - 8 oz Onions	½ tsp Salt and pepper
2 Garlic cloves, finely chopped	2 tbsp Honey
1 tbsp Smoked paprika	1 Lemon, juice and grated zest
1 tbsp Ground cumin	

1. Preheat the oven to 200°C, gas mark 6.

2. Heat some oil in a frying pan, slice the onions and add to the pan with the spare ribs and fry for a few minutes until golden. Place in a roasting pan in a single layer.

3. Put the garlic, paprika, cumin, ginger, salt and pepper in a bowl and mix together. Coat both sides of each rib with equal amounts of the mixture.

4. Squeeze the juice of the lemon and grate the rind in a small pan add the honey and heat over a low heat for a 3 - 4 minutes, allow to boil for 1 minute. Spoon half of the honey glaze over the spare ribs.

5. Bake in the oven for 10 minutes, then turn the ribs and spoon over the remaining glaze. Bake for a further 10 minutes.

6. Serve on a bed of rice with mixed vegetables.

Roast Loin Of Pork With Special Honey Apple Sauce

Serves 4 - 6

1 kg - 2½ lb Joint of pork loin	15 g - ½ oz Butter
Pepper and salt	1 dsp Honey

1. Preheat the oven to 200°C, gas mark 6.

2. Season the joint with the pepper and salt.

3. In an oven proof dish heat the butter and honey, add the meat and brown on all sides. Place the dish in the preheated oven and cook for about 50 minutes per 1 kg 22 minutes per 1lb, baste the loin with it cooking juices several times during cooking.

4. Make a gravy with the cooking juices by blending corn flour and some water from the cooked vegetables of your choice. Mix well over a gentle heat to thicken.

5. Serve with potatoes which can be either plain boiled, mashed, roasted or dauphinoise.

3 Apples,	4 tbsp Honey
60 ml Orange juice	1 tsp Lemon juice

The Honey Apple Sauce:
Granny Smith apples make a perfect sauce. However, you could also use Bramley's but you will require more honey to sweeten.

1. Peel core and chop the apples. Put all the ingredients in a food processor and blend to the desired consistency.

2. If using Bramley cooking apples pre-cook them until just slightly soft.

Lamb Shanks With Honey

Serves 4

4 Lamb shanks	250 ml - 8 fl oz Red wine
50 g - 2 oz Butter	1 tbsp Worcester sauce
2 Onions, peeled and sliced	2 tbsp Honey
5 Garlic cloves, crushed	2 tsp Cayenne pepper
1 Orange, juiced and grated zest	1 tbsp Fresh rosemary, chopped
250 g - 8 fl oz Meat stock	Pepper and salt

1. Preheat the oven to 150°C, gas mark 2.

2. Melt the butter in a pan over a medium heat add the meat and brown on both sides. Remove to a roasting tin leaving the juices in the pan.

3. Add the onions, garlic and orange juice and zest to the pan and cook until just soft before adding the red wine, Worcester sauce, honey, cayenne pepper, stock , pepper and salt. Stir and simmer for 5 minutes. Pour over the meat in the roasting tin and sprinkle the rosemary on top, cover and place in the oven, cook slowly for 3 hours.

4. Remove the lamb shanks onto a serving dish. The sauce left in the pan can be thickened with a little corn flour and poured over the meat.

5. Serve hot with rice and a salad.

Chicken Thighs With Lemon, Honey And Potato Wedges

Serves 6

12 Chicken thighs, with skins	:	2 tsp Honey
1 Red onion	:	2 tbsp Oive oil
550 g - 1¼ lb Potatoes	:	Salt and pepper
1 Lemon	:	1 tsp Fresh thyme
6 Garlic cloves	:	6 Sprigs fresh rosemary

1. Preheat the oven to 200°C, gas mark 6.

2. Dry fry the chicken thighs in a non stick pan for 2 - 3 minutes until brown. Place in a large roasting tin.

3. Cut each of the onions into 8 wedges and the potatoes into many thin wedges and add it all to the pan. Grate the zest from the lemon and set aside. Cut the lemon in half, slice one half into 4 and add to the pan with 4 whole clove of garlic.

4. Squeeze the juice from the other half of the lemon into a dish and mix with the zest, honey, oil. Crush the remaining 2 garlic cloves and add to the dish. Pour over the chicken and season. Finally add the herbs.

5. Bake for 35 - 40 minutes or until the wedges are tender and the chicken is cooked. Remove the sprigs of rosemary and serve immediately.

Honeyed Lamb And Vegetable Stir - Fry

Serves 4

400 g – 14 oz Lamb fillets thinly sliced
2 tbsp Ground nut oil
1 Garlic clove, crushed
1 Large onion, thinly sliced
1 Large carrot, thinly sliced
1 Large red pepper, sliced
3 Small courgettes, cut into chunks

425 g - 15 oz Can sweetcorn, drained
125 g - 4 oz French beans
1 tbsp Cornflour
3 tbsp Light soy sauce
2 tbsp water
1 tbsp Honey

1. Heat half of the oil in a wok or large frying pan. Stir-fry the lamb and garlic until the lamb is browned, then set a side.

2. Prepare the vegetables: thinly slice the onion and carrots, cut the pepper into strip and courgette small chunks. Drain the can of sweetcorn and halve the French beans. Heat the remaining oil in the pan and add the onion and carrot until just softened, then add the courgette, pepper and beans. Stir-fry until all the vegetables are just tender finally adding the sweetcorn. Stir or toss well to combine.

3. Return the lamb to the pan, mix well. Make the sauce by blending the cornflour with the soy sauce, water and honey, stir into the meat and vegetables until the mixture boils and thickens slightly.

4. Serve immediately.

Honey Chicken And Noodle Stir - Fry

Serves 4

4 Skinless chicken breasts · 2 tbsp Fresh ginger, grated
225 g - 8 oz Broccoli · 250 g - 9 oz Chinese egg noodles
1 Large red onion · 3 tbsp Light soy sauce
1 Large red pepper · 2 tbsp Lemon juice
150 g - 6 oz Sweetcorn, tinned or frozen · 2 tbsp Honey
2 tbsp Sesame oil · Salt to taste
2 tbsp Ground nut oil · 50 g - 2 oz Cashew nuts
2 Cloves garlic, finely chopped · 2 tbsp Sesame seeds, toasted
1 Small red chilli, seeded and chopped ·

1. Put a pan of water on to heat for cooking the noodles.

2. Cut the chicken in to thin strips, and the broccoli into small florets. Heat the oil in a wok or large frying pan. Add the chicken and stir fry over a high heat for 5 minutes or until brown.

3. Cut the red onion in thin slices and add to the pan with the broccoli florets and pepper, cook for a further few minutes before adding the garlic, chilli, ginger, and sweet corn, cook for 3 - 4 minutes.

4. Put the noodles in the pan of boiling water and cook as stated on he packet. Add the soy sauce, lemon juice and honey to the stir fry and allow to bubble through for a minute or two. Add the salt to taste and the nuts. Drain the noodles and stir through the mixture.

5. Sprinkle the sesame seeds over and serve immediately.

Ginger And Turkey Meatballs With Honey Sauce

Serves 4

4 Skinless turkey breasts, chopped
4 Spring onions, chopped
2 Garlic cloves, roughly chopped

½ tbsp Fresh thyme leaves
2.5 cm - 1 inch Root ginger, peeled and grated

For the Sauce:
1 tbsp Honey
1 tbsp Soy sauce

1 tsp Sesame oil
1 tsp Lemon juice

1. Preheat a grill to a medium heat and place the rack about 10 cm - 4 inch away from the heat. Grease a large baking tray.

2. Put the chopped turkey into a food processor and whiz until it resembles mince. Add the spring onions, garlic, thyme, and ginger and whiz again briefly to combine. Form the turkey mixture into golf ball size meat balls. There should be about 16, and arrange on the baking tray.

3. Grill the meat balls for 10 - 15 minutes, turning once, until golden and cooked through.

4. In a small bowl mix together all the ingredients for the pouring sauce. Add 1 tbsp of water.

5. Serve the meat balls with the pouring sauce and some cooked wild rice.

Crispy Duck With Honey And Mead

Serves 6

6 Plump duck legs
6 tbsp Honey
1 Bramley apple, peeled, cored and chopped
5 cm - 2 inch Root ginger, peeled and grated
1 tsp Ground cinnamon
300 ml - ½ pint Mead or cider

300 ml - ½ pint Light stock e.g vegetable
1 Orange, grated zest
3 Garlic cloves
3 tbsp Balsamic vinegar
1 tbsp Sea salt

1. Preheat the oven to 170°C, gas mark 3.

2. Place the duck legs skin side down in a flameproof roasting tin large enough to hold them in one layer. Add 4 tbsp of the honey, plus the apple, ginger, cinnamon, mead, stock, garlic and the juice and zest of the orange. Bring to the boil. Cook over a medium heat for 3 minutes, then cover with foil and transfer to the oven for 2½ hours.

3. When cooked skim off the fat which can be kept in a jar in the fridge for 2 weeks.

4. Remove the duck legs onto a baking sheet skin side up. Strain the cooking juices into a pan and bring to the boil. Reduce by half.

5. Turn the oven temperature up to 220°C, gas mark 7.

6. Mix the vinegar and remaining 2 tbsp of honey together and brush over the duck legs. Rub the sea salt into the skin. Place uncovered in the oven for 15 minutes. Warm the sauce and serve with the duck. Complete the meal with crushed new potatoes and seasonal vegetables.

Chicken Marinated In Honey And Mead

Serves 4

4 Chicken breasts   2 tbsp Mead or sherry
1 Egg white   1 tsp Soy sauce
1 Lemon, finely grated   2 tsp Honey
3 tbsp Ground nut oil

1. Put the egg white into a bowl and whisk until frothy. Mix in the grated lemon rind and juice, mead, oil, soy sauce and honey. Place the chicken in the marinade and cover with cling film. Put in the refrigerator for several hours or over night.

2. Remove any excess liquid from the chicken and either cook on a barbecue, turning gently until golden brown, or place on a baking tray and cook in a hot oven for about 30 minutes until cooked through.

3. Serve with a salad and a pasta dish of your choice.

Chicken With Honey Lemon Sauce

Serves 4

4 Chicken breasts	6 tbsp Chicken stock
2 Egg whites	1 Lemon
2 tbsp Soy sauce	5 cm - 2 inch Root ginger, peeled and grated
125 g - 4 oz Cornflour	2 tbsp Cornflour, extra
Sprinkle of olive oil	1 tbsp Sherry
6 tbsp Honey	

1. Preheat the oven to 200°C, gas mark 6. Grease a large baking tray.

2. Cut each chicken breast into 3 - 4 slices following the grain of the meat.

3. Put the egg whites and soy sauce in a mixing bowl and whisk until the mixture starts to foam. Spread the cornflour onto a dish. Place the chicken into the egg white mixture and stir with a folk to coat. Remove the chicken pieces from the egg white mixture and place in the dish of flour coating thoroughly.

4. Place the chicken pieces on the prepared baking tray and sprinkle with a little olive oil. Bake for 10 - 15 minutes or until the chicken pieces are cooked through and crispy.

5. Place the honey, chicken stock, juice of the lemon and grated ginger into a small pan. Stir to combine and bring slowly to the boil then reduce to a simmer. Simmer uncovered for 3 - 4 minutes.

6. Blend the extra cornflour with the sherry and add to the honey mixture, stir until the mixture comes to a boil again, then reduce to a simmer for a further 3 - 4 minutes.

7. Serve with rice or pasta and vegetables of your choice.

Oriental Honeyed Pork Or Chicken

Serves 4

335 g - 12 oz Pork fillet or 4 chicken breasts · 1 Yellow pepper, chopped
3 dsp Seasoned flour · 225 g - 8 oz Tin of pineapple chunks
6 tbsp Ground nut oil · 3 Large mushrooms, sliced
1 Garlic clove, crushed · 2 Large tomatoes, cut into quarters

For the Sauce: · 1 tbsp Soy sauce
1 Chicken stock cube · 2 tbsp Honey
300 ml - ½ pint Boiling water ·

1. Cut the pork or chicken into cubes and coat with half the flour.

2. In a large pan heat the garlic in the oil and fry the meat on a medium heat until brown on all sides. Lower the heat and add the chopped pepper and sliced mushrooms. Cook slowly for about 10 minutes. Add the tomatoes and the pineapple chunks, reserving the juice. Cook for a further 10 minutes. Transfer to a warm serving dish.

3. Next make the sauce.
In a saucepan dissolve the stoke cube in boiling water, add the soy sauce and honey, mix well. Blend the rest of the seasoned flour with a little of the remaining pineapple juice and add to the stock mixture stirring well. Bring to the boil and cook for 3 minutes stirring all the time.

4. Pour over the meat and serve with rice and vegetables or a salad.

St. David's Day Chicken With Honeyed Leeks

This is a swift and simple dish that I have cooked to celebrate this special day. It is a delicately flavoured meal that can also be served in different ways, such as with boiled rice or pasta.

Serves 4

4 Chicken Breasts	300 ml - ½ pint Double cream
675 g - 1½ lb Welsh leeks	Juice of half a lemon
75 g - 10 oz Butter	¼ tsp Grated nutmeg,
1 tsp Honey	Salt and cayenne Pepper
2 Egg yolks	Chopped Parsley to garnish

1. Cut the chicken breasts into fairly thin slices. Wash the leeks, remove the green tops and cut across in 1cm - ½ inch rings.

2. Melt 25 g - 1 oz of the butter in a large frying pan. Add the sliced chicken and cook for 10 minutes making sure the chicken is thoroughly done. Transfer to a covered dish and keep warm in a low oven.

3. Add the remaining 50 g - 2 oz butter and the honey to the pan juices and melt. Add the sliced leeks and stir over a gentle heat for 6 - 10 minutes until soft. Remove the leeks from the pan and put them with the chicken, leaving the juices in the pan.

4. Whisk the egg yolks together with the cream and pour into the pan. Just heat gently for a minute or two, stirring all the time but do not boil. Gradually add the lemon juice, still stirring constantly. Add the grated nutmeg, salt and cayenne pepper to taste. Mix the sauce in with the chicken and leeks.

5. Serve with new Pembrokeshire potatoes and early spring vegetables.

Fish Recipes

From a Welsh Kitchen

Baked Sea Bass With Honey And Lemongrass

Serves 4

1 Whole sea bass about 1.4 kg - 3 lb	3 cm - 1 inch Root ginger
3 Lemongrass stalks	1 dsp Honey
2 Small chillies	2 tbsp Olive oil
2 Garlic cloves, sliced	1 Lime

1. Preheat the oven to 200°C, gas mark 6.

2. Gut and clean the sea bass, then wash inside and out, and pat dry with kitchen paper. Score across the fish and through the skin 4 - 5 times on each side, then lay the fish on a large piece of oiled foil, big enough to wrap it up loosely.

3. Cut the lemongrass stalks diagonally and peel and cut the ginger into small pieces. Put the lemongrass, chillies, garlic and ginger into a mortar with the honey, 1 tbsp of the oil and squeeze in the juice of the lime. Bash it several times with the pestle until everything is bruised, there is no need to grind it finely. Season the fish inside and out. Spread half the pounded mixture into the cavity. Add the remaining oil to the mortar, and mix again. Rub over the fish making sure it penetrates the score lines on both sides. Pull the sides of the foil up to create a loose parcel. Crimp the edges to seal, making sure there is some space around the fish.

4. Bake for 25 minutes. Rest for 5 minutes before opening the parcel.
This dish is a good accompaniment when served with honey roasted vegetables and couscous,(see the chapter on vegetarian dishes).

Cod With Coconut And Honey

Serves 4

4 x 150 g - 5 oz Cod loins	150 ml - 5 fl oz Coconut cream
1 Medium red chilli, deseeded	1 tsp Turmeric
2 Garlic cloves	2 tbsp Fresh coriander, chopped
5 Spring onions	Salt and pepper
1 tbsp Honey	

1. Preheat the grill to a medium temperature.

2. Put the chilli in a processor with the garlic, spring onions, honey, coconut cream, turmeric and coriander, season and whiz until almost smooth.

3. Cut two slashes in each piece of cod. Put them on a baking tray, then spoon half the marinade over the top. Grill for 3 - 4 minutes.

4. Turn the cod over, spread the remaining marinade evenly on top and cook for a further 3 - 4 minutes.

5. Serve with warm naan bread, a wedge of lemon to squeeze over and an avocado, chick pea and red onion salad.

6. In a bowl mix together a drained can of chick peas with slices of red onion and slices of avocado, season and drizzle with oil and a little honey to taste.

Salmon Fillet Baked With Lemon And Honey

There are many different sauces containing honey that can be used with fish.
The combination of lemon and honey in a light sauce with salmon is particularly good.
Always choose wild salmon over farmed, as it has more flavour.

Serves 8

50 g - 2 oz Unsalted butter
2. 5 kg - 5lb Salmon fillet
Salt and ground pepper
200 ml - 7 fl oz Crème fraiche
30 g - 1 oz Fresh dill, chopped

15 g - ½ oz Fresh mint, chopped
2 Lemons, zest finely grated
1 tbsp Honey
Sprigs of dill and lemon slices to garnish

1. Preheat the oven to 190°C, gas mark 5.
Grease a large baking tray.

2. Place the salmon on the baking tray skin side down. Dot with the butter and
season with salt and pepper. Bake for 20 minutes.

3. In a bowl mix together the crème fraiche, dill, mint, lemon zest, honey and a little
salt. Spread the mixture down the centre of the salmon and return to the oven for
a further 10 minutes or until the sauce has melted and the fish is cooked through.
Check by piercing the thickest part of the fillet with the tip of a knife.

4. Transfer to a warmed serving plate and spoon the sauce from the baking tray over
the fish and serve garnished with the sprigs of dill and slices of lemon.

5. Serve with new potatoes and a green salad.

Trout With Honey And Ginger Marinade And Honey Dressing With Noodles

Serves 4

4 Trout fillets	10 Spring onions, sliced diagonally
125 g - 4 oz Egg noodles	Sprigs of mint to garnish
½ Cucumber, cut into matchsticks	

For the Marinade:
1 tsp Honey	1 tbsp Sesame seeds
2 tbsp Soy sauce	1 Garlic clove, crushed
	2. 5 cm - 1 inch Fresh root ginger

For the Dressing:
2 tbsp Wine vinegar	1 tbsp Soy sauce
1 tsp Honey	1 tbsp Sunflower oil
1 tbsp Sesame oil	1 cm - ½ inch Fresh root ginger

1. Peel and grate the root ginger. Combine all the marinade ingredients in a large but shallow dish, then add the trout fillets. Coat both sides in the mixture, cover and leave to marinate for 1 hour in the fridge.

2. Again, peel and grate the root ginger, then whisk together the dressing ingredients. Put on one side.

3. Heat a large frying pan and gently cook the fillets for 3 - 4 minutes on each side.

4. Meanwhile, boil the noodles according to the packet instructions, then drain well. Toss with the dressing, cucumber pieces and spring onions.

5. Divide between 4 plates, top with the fish and garnish with fresh mint.

Mackerel With Honey And Herb Stuffing

Mackerel makes a cost effective meal, but they need to be fresh.
Try to buy bright stiff-looking fish rather than flabby and tired-looking ones.

Serves 4

4 Mackerel fillets	100g - 3½ oz Fresh tarragon, chopped
1 tbsp Mustard, Dijon or whole grain	3 tsp Lemon juice
1 tbsp Honey	25 g - 1 oz Butter
1 tbsp Snipped chives	50g - 2 oz White breadcrumbs
100g - 3½ oz Fresh parsley, chopped	Salt and pepper

1. Preheat the oven to 190°C, gas mark 5.

2. Wash and dry the mackerel thoroughly.

3. The mackerel should be gutted and have their heads removed. Mix together the mustard, honey, parsley, tarragon, chives and lemon juice in a bowl. Melt the butter in a frying pan then stir in the breadcrumbs and season with salt and pepper. Add to all the other ingredients in the bowl combining well together.

4. Pack an equal quantity of the mixture into the belly of each fish. Place them on a large baking tray and cover with greased foil, making sure the edges are tightly sealed.

5. Cook for 25 - 30 minutes or until cooked through.
Serve with mashed potatoes and some freshly cooked spinach.

Honey And Mandarin Swordfish

Serves 4

4 Fresh Swordfish steaks
Mandarin segments for decoration

50 g - 2 oz Spring onions, chopped

For the Marinade:
4 tbsp Soy sauce
4 tbsp Mandarin juice
2.5cm - 1 inch Root ginger, crushed

3 tbsp Honey
1 tbsp Sesame oil
3 Garlic cloves, crushed

1. Place all the marinade ingredients into a mixing bowl and whisk to combine.

2. Add the swordfish to the marinade and cover. Put in the fridge for an hour, turning once or twice.

3. Preheat a grill to high. Lift the fish out of the marinade, then strain the liquid in to a small saucepan, add the ginger and boil to a thick syrupy glaze.

4. Lightly brush the swordfish with oil and also oil the grill plate. Grill the fish for 5 minutes on each side.

5. Remove to a serving plate and pour over the marinade. Sprinkle the spring onions on top with the Mandarin segments for decoration. Serve with new potatoes and seasonal vegetables.

Haddock With Honey Soy Dressing

Serves 4

4 Thick white haddock fillets	1 tbsp olive oil
For the Dressing:	1 tbsp Sesame oil
2 tbsp Soy sauce	Pinch of ground black pepper
2 tbsp Honey	50 ml - 2 fl oz Water
2 tbsp balsamic vinegar	

1. In a small bowl mix all these ingredients for the dressing together.

2. Heat the olive oil for 1 minute in a non - stick frying pan with a lid. Add the fish and cover. Cook for 3 minutes. Remove the cover and turn the fish carefully.

3. Add the dressing and cover again. Turn down the heat and cook for a further 3 minutes. Remove from the heat and rest for a few minutes before serving.

4. This is a healthy low fat meal and is delicious served with rice or a salad.

Salmon With Dill And Honey Sauce

Serves 4

4 Welsh salmon steaks	25 g - 1 oz Butter
1 Lemon, cut into slices	
For the Sauce:	2 tbsp Lime juice
225 g - 8 oz Greek style yoghurt	2 tbsp Honey
2 tbsp Fresh Dill, chopped	Salt and Pepper
2 tbsp Fresh chives, chopped	

1. Preheat the grill to high.

2. Place the salmon steaks in the grill pan and top with a little butter on each steak. Arrange the lemon slices along the top and season with salt and pepper.
Grill for 6 - 8 minutes until cooked through. There is no need to turn the steaks.

3. In a bowl, mix together the yoghurt, dill, chives, lime juice and honey.
Season to taste.

4. The sauce can be served either warm or cold. To warm the sauce, heat gently but do not boil, because it will separate. Stir continuously.

5. Drizzle the sauce over the salmon steaks and serve with new potatoes, green beans and a wedge of fresh lemon or lime to garnish.

Sauce For Salmon

The following recipe is a chunky sauce that can also be used as a side dish.
Serves 4

1 Small cucumber	1 Lime, juice and zest
1 Orange, thinly sliced	1 tbsp Sesame seeds
1 Yellow pepper, thinly sliced	2 tbsp Honey
12 Cherry tomatoes, halved	1 tbsp Whole grain mustard
3 Spring onions, thinly sliced	Salt and pepper

1. Halve the cucumber lengthways, then scoop out the seeds with a teaspoon and discard. Cut each half into small diagonal slices and put into a bowl. Add the peppers, tomatoes and half the spring onions.

2. Mix together the lime zest and juice, sesame seeds, honey and mustard. Add a splash of water, season, then pour over the vegetables and toss together.

Vegetarian And Salad Recipes

From a Welsh Kitchen

Autumn Flan With Honey, Cheese And Walnuts

Honey is frequently used in recipes using cheese. This flan using Welsh brie makes a perfect combination.

Serves 6

The Short Crust Pastry: | 1 Egg yolk
225 g - 8 oz plain flour | Pinch of salt
125 g - 4 oz Butter

The Filling: | 3 tbsp Honey
300 g - 11 oz Welsh brie | Salt and pepper
2 Apples, a firm eating variety is preferable | 4 Eggs
100 g - 3½ oz Walnuts | 200 g - 7 oz Double cream
1 Onion | Nutmeg

1. Preheat the oven to 200°C, gas mark 6.
A loose bottom flan tin 35 cm - 14 inches.

2. Sift the flour and salt in to a bowl, cut the butter into small pieces and mix into the flour with your finger tips to resemble fine breadcrumbs. This can also be done in a food processor.

3. Mix the egg yolk with a little water and add to the mixture, combine together to make a soft, but dry dough. Remember at this point that the more water you use, the more the pastry will shrink when you bake it blind. Roll out on a floured surface and line the flan tin. Cover the bottom with a circle of greaseproof paper and top with cooking beans. Bake blind for 20 minutes.

4. Cut the apple into small slices and finely chop the onion. Fry gently in a little oil until soft and brown. Add the honey and salt and pepper to taste.

5. Cut the Brie into small pieces and with the walnuts place in the pastry lined flan tin. Cover with the cooked mixture of apples and onions. Beat the eggs with the cream add a pinch of nutmeg and pour into the tart.

6. Reduce the oven temperature to 180°C, gas mark 4 and cook for 45 minutes until lightly brown and firm to touch.

Glamorgan Sausages

These vegetarian sausages are also known as Selsig Morgannwg. They are made with lots of cheese and are very popular with non - vegetarians as well.

Serves 4

1 Large onion, finely sliced	2 Celery sticks, finely chopped
1 tbsp Honey	3 Eggs
450 g - 16 oz Breadcrumbs	1½ tsp English mustard
550 g - 1½ lb Caerphilly cheese	4 tbsp Olive oil
25 g - 1 oz Parsley, finely chopped	

1. Add a little of the oil to a frying pan and gently fry the onions until just soft. Just before they finish cooking drizzle with the honey. Tip into a large bowl. Finely chop or crumble the cheese and add to the bowl along with 400 g / 14 oz of the breadcrumbs, the parsley and the celery. Beat together the eggs and mustard and add two - thirds to the bowl. Mix well to combine.

2. Divide the mixture into 12 and shape each portion into a chunky sausage. Put the remaining beaten egg mixture and breadcrumbs onto two separate plates. Dip each sausage into the egg mixture, then into the breadcrumbs. Arrange on a plate and chill for 30 minutes.

3. Heat the remaining oil in a frying pan and fry the sausages in batches for 10 minutes until golden, turning occasionally.

4. Serve with a green salad and your favourite chutney.

Honey Roast Corn On The Cob

Corn on the cob is usually served with lots of butter. Enjoy them just as much with a sticky coating of sweet honey. They make an ideal accompaniment for the leek terrine.

Serves 4

4 Large corn on the cob	2 tbsp Honey
1 Vegetable stock cube	Salt and pepper
1 litre - 2 pints Water	Chives, a few freshly chopped
1 tsp Cumin powder	

1. Preheat the oven to 200°C, gas mark 6.

2. Remove the outer husks and silky threads from the cobs of corn and trim the end with a sharp knife.

3. In a large saucepan dissolve the stock cube in the water. Add the cumin powder and bring to the boil. Carefully add the corn making sure they are completely covered. Simmer for 10 - 15 minutes.

4. Drain through a colander and place on a roasting tray. Drizzle with honey and season with salt and pepper.

5. Place in the oven for 15 - 20 minutes until lightly roasted. Serve hot with a sprinkling of chopped fresh chives.

Honey Roasted Vegetable Couscous

Serves 4

3 Fennel bulbs	3 Red peppers
3 Red onions	2 tbsp Honey
7 tbsp Olive oil	Salt and pepper
700 g - 1½ lb Aubergines	1 x 500 g Packet couscous
700 g - 1½ lb Courgettes	

1. Preheat the oven to 240°C, gas mark 9.

2. Cut the fennel and onions into wedges and place in two large roasting tins. Mix 2 tbsp of oil into each batch. Cook in the oven for 15 minutes.

3. Meanwhile, cut the aubergines, courgettes and red peppers into large pieces. Divide between the two roasting tins containing the fennel and onions. Drizzle with 1 tbsp of oil and1 tbsp of honey, season with salt and pepper and mix together.

4. Cook for 50 - 55 minutes, or until golden brown and tender, turn the vegetables from time to time.

5. When cooked remove from the oven and leave to cool.

6. Put the couscous in a bowl with a pinch of salt and the remaining oil. Pour on 600 ml - 1 pint boiling water, cover and leave to stand for 10 minutes.

7. Put the couscous in a serving dish and place the roasted vegetable on top, drizzle with a little more oil and 1 tbsp of honey.

8. This is a recipe that can be served with most fish dishes.

Honey Roast Squash With Vegetables And Couscous

Serves 4

2 Butternut squash	1 Red pepper
5 tbsp Olive oil	100 g - 3½ oz Mushrooms
3 tbsp Honey	2 Garlic cloves
100 g - 3½ oz Couscous	150 g - 5 oz Walnuts, chopped
1 Red onion	1 tbsp Fresh parsley, finely chopped
1 Medium courgette	Salt and pepper

1. Preheat the oven to 200°C, gas mark 6.

2. Cut the squash in half, lengthways. Using a spoon scoop out the seeds and part of the flesh from the squash. It needs quite a deep hollow to allow plenty of room for the filling. Discard the seeds but any flesh can be kept and added to the other ingredients for the filling.

3. Mix 3 tbsp of olive oil with the honey and brush this over the inside of the squash. Place the 4 halves cut side up on a baking tray. Roast the squash in the middle of the oven for 30 - 35 minutes until tender.

4. Meanwhile put the couscous in a bowl and add boiling water according to the instructions on the packet.

5. To prepare the vegetables, finally chop the red onion, cut the courgette into small chunks, deseed and finally chop the red pepper, and chop the mushroom. Heat the remaining oil in a large frying pan until just sizzling, then add all the vegetables and the garlic. Fry over a gentle heat stirring occasionally for 10 minutes until just tender.

6. Remove from the heat and add the walnuts and parsley. Season and stir well. Add the prepared couscous and combine together. After the squash has cooked for around 30 minutes, spoon equal portions into the 4 halves and return to the oven for 15 minutes until golden brown.

7. Remove from the oven and place on a serving dish. Either drizzle a little extra honey over the squash or top with grated parmesan cheese.

Leek Terrine With Honey And Mustard Vinaigrette

Serves 4

1 kg - 2 lb Leeks	Salt and pepper
50 g - 2 oz Butter	For the Vinaigrette
1 tsp Honey	1 tbsp Honey
3 tbsp Chives, roughly chopped	1 tbsp Dijon mustard
3 tbsp White wine	1 tsp Peppercorns
3 tbsp Pink peppercorns	2 tbsp White wine vinegar
6 tbsp Single cream	6 tbsp Olive oil
1 tsp Dijon mustard	Black pepper, freshly ground
2 Eggs	

1. Preheat the oven to 175°C, gas mark 4.

2. Trim 4 of the leeks to fit lengthways in a 1 litre - 1 pint loaf tin. Cover with boiling water and cook for 2 - 3 minutes until they start turning colour and slightly softened. Remove them from the tin and plunge them into cold water to stop the cooking process. Pat them with kitchen paper and set aside.

3. Grease the loaf tin.

4. Slice the remaining leeks into rounds, melt the butter and honey in a frying pan, add the sliced leeks and cook for 4 - 5 minutes until tender. Allow to cool slightly the place in a food processor with the chopped chives, white wine, peppercorn, cream, mustard, eggs and salt and pepper. Process for 30 seconds until the leeks are roughly chopped.

5. Place half the chopped leek mixture in the bottom of the greased tin, arrange the four leeks on top and pour the remaining mixture on top. Cover with foil and place in a deep baking tray with enough water to come half way up the tin. Place in the oven and bake for 45 - 50 minutes or until set.

6. To make the vinaigrette, place all the ingredients in a jug, stir well until well combined.

7. Remove the terrine from the oven and allow to cool. Carefully run a knife around the edge of the tin and tip the terrine onto the serving plate.

8. Serve with the vinaigrette, new potatoes and honey roasted corn on the cob.

Spring Salad With Honey And Caramelised Walnuts

Serves 6

50 g - 2 oz Walnut halves	2 tbsp Olive oil
2 tbsp Honey	2 Large oranges
2 Thick slices sourdough bread	200 g - 7 oz mixed salad leaves
1 tbsp Mustard	100 g - 3½ oz Radishes, thickly sliced
2 tbsp Balsamic vinegar	125 g - 4 oz Goats cheese

1. Preheat the oven to 180°C, gas mark 6.
A large baking sheet lined with greaseproof paper.

2. Mix the walnuts with 1 tbsp of honey. Spread them on half of the baking sheet. Cut the bread into cubes and scatter on the other half and drizzle with a little oil. Cook in the oven for 12 - 15 minutes, turning both halfway through.

3. Put the remaining honey, mustard, vinegar and oil into a small pan. Season and stir over a gentle heat, do not boil.

4. Meanwhile peel the oranges and slice into segments cutting between the membranes. Place the orange segments into a large bowl. Add the croutons, salad leaves, radishes and goats cheese to the bowl with the orange segments, and toss to combine.

5. Arrange the salad on six plates and drizzle with the warm dressing. Finally garnish with the honey toasted walnuts to serve.

Summer Salad With Feta Cheese And Honey Dressing

Serves 4

1 Large packet of mixed salad	2 Small courgettes
2 x 410 g Tins chickpeas	50 g - 2 oz Raisins
4 Tomatoes	1 tsp Honey
1 Red onion	2 x 200g - 7 oz packets of feta cheese

For The Dressing:

1 tbsp Whole grain mustard	2 tbsp Extra virgin olive oil
2 tsp Honey	Large handful of basil
1 tsp White wine vinegar	2 tbsp Pumpkin seeds

1. Arrange the salad in the bottom of the serving bowl.
Drain and rinse the chickpeas, roughly chop the tomatoes, thinly slice the red onion and cut the courgettes into ribbons using a potato peeler. Place all these ingredients, along with the raisins into a large serving bowl.

2. Roughly break up the feta cheese and crumble on top of the salad. Drizzle the teaspoon of honey over the cheese and salad.

3. In a small jug, whisk together the mustard, honey, vinegar, oil and some seasoning. Pour over the salad and toss to coat.

4. Sprinkle with the basil and pumpkin seeds and serve immediately.

Autumn Salad With Chicken And A Spicy Pumpkin and Honey Dressing

Serves 6

50 g - 2 oz Watercress	150 g - 5 oz Green olives, stoned and halved
50 g - 2 oz Rocket	200g - 7 oz Cooked chicken pieces
25 g - 1 oz Each of Walnuts,	2 x 400g Tins mixed salad beans
25 g - 1 oz Pine nuts	1 tsp honey
25 g - 1 oz Pumpkin seeds	

For The Dressing:
50 g - 2 oz Pumpkin seeds	1 tbsp Lemon juice
1 - 2 Pinches dried chilli flakes	1 tsp Honey
3 tbsp Extra virgin olive oil	½ tsp Whole grain mustard

1. In a large bowl mix together the salad leaves, all the nuts and the olives. Drain the liquid from the tins of beans, pour into another bowl and stir in the honey before transferring to the large bowl of salad. At this point the salad can either be divided among the six serving plates or kept as one large dish. Finally add the cooked chicken.

2. Heat a frying pan and toast the pumpkin seeds over a medium heat for 1 - 2 minutes until lightly browned. Tip into a small bowl and leave to cool. In a separate small bowl, whisk together the chilli flakes, oil, lemon juice, honey, mustard and some seasoning.

3. When ready to serve the salad, sprinkle the toasted pumpkin seeds evenly over the top of the salad and finish with a drizzle of the spicy dressing.

Winter Salad With Turkey And A Honey And Mustard Vinaigrette

Serves 4

550 g - 1¼ oz Baby new potatoes
200 g - 7 oz Baby spinach leaves
100 g - 3½ oz Mixed salad leaves
200 g - 7 oz Green beans, trimmed
2 Small carrots, grated

1 Red pepper, seeded and cut into strips
4 Tomatoes, quartered
400 g - 14 oz cooked turkey
½ Red onion, peeled and finely sliced
1 tsp honey

For The Vinaigrette:
3 tbsp Honey
5 tbsp Extra virgin olive oil
6 tbsp Mayonnaise

1 tbsp White wine vinegar
2 tbsp Chopped parsley
1 dsp Shallot, finely chopped
2 tbsp Smooth prepared mustard

1. Wash and halve the potatoes and boil for about 15 minutes until tender. Drain and leave on one side to cool. Steam the green beans for about 10 minutes, or until just tender.

2. Divide the salad leaves, beans, tomatoes, carrot, pepper between 4 plates. Cut the cooled potatoes into small chunks and add to the salads. Top with equal amounts of turkey. Mix the slices of red onion with the teaspoon of honey and sprinkle on top of each plate.

3. To make the vinaigrette, mix all the ingredients together in a bowl until smooth and creamy. Serve in a separate jug or pour a little over each salad.

4. This dish can also be made as one large salad.

Warm Winter Salad With Honey And Vegetables

Serves 4

3 tbsp Oregano, freshly chopped
75 ml Ground nut oil
1 ½ tbsp Honey
1 tbsp Dijon mustard
Salt and pepper

For The Dressing:
75 ml Balsamic vinegar
2 tsp Dijon mustard

550 g - 1 ¼ lb Swede, cut into chunks
300 g - 11 oz Chantenary carrots
1 Red onion, cut into wedged
3 Chicken breasts, with skin on
200 g - 7 oz Spinach leaves

1 dsp Honey
1 dsp Cold water

1. Preheat the oven to 200°C, gas mark 6.

2. In a large bowl, mix together the oregano, oil, honey, salt and pepper, and half the mustard. Add the swede, carrots and onion, and toss to coat. Tip into a roasting tin and cook for 35 - 40 minutes until tender and golden.

3. Heat 1 teaspoon of oil in a frying pan and gently fry the chicken breasts, skin-side down, for 10 minutes so that the skin is crisp and dark golden. Turn the chicken over and fry for another 5 - 10 minutes until cooked through and the juices run clear when the meat is pierced with a knife. Thinly slice the chicken breasts and keep warm.

4. Whisk all the dressing ingredients together.

5. Arrange the spinach leaves in a serving dish and top with the vegetables and sliced chicken. Drizzle with the dressing.

Dessert Recipes

From a Welsh Kitchen

Snowdon Pudding

Serves 8

100 g - 4 oz Raisins • 2 tbsp Welsh honey
225 g - 8 oz Suet • 225 g - 8 oz Breadcrumbs
1 heaped tsp Cornflour • 2 lemons, the rind grated
100 g - 4 oz Soft brown sugar • 6 eggs

1. Preheat the oven to 190°C, gas mark 5.
Grease eight ramekins or pudding moulds and dot the inside with some of the raisins.

2. Mix all the dry ingredients together, then add the honey. Beat the eggs and stir into the mixture. Mix well so that everything is well combined together. Divide the mixture between the ramekins.

3. Place on a baking tray, pour about 5 cm - 2 inches of boiling water around the moulds. Cover with greased foil. Bake for about 40 minutes.

For the Sauce: • 2 lemons, juiced
2 tbsp Lemon marmalade • 2 tbsp Welsh honey
2 tbsp Thinly sliced lemon peel •

To make the sauce:
1. Place the lemon marmalade in a pan together with the lemon peel, juice and honey. Bring to a fast boil and cook until syrupy. Turn the puddings out and drizzle with the sauce.

2. Serve with custard, cream or yoghurt.

Chocolate And Honey Pecan Tart

This tart is a variation on an old favourite with a distinct taste of honey. The best honey to use for this recipe is one which is of a thick consistency and with a strong flavour such as chestnut.

Serves 6 - 8

For the Pastry:
125 g - 4 oz Butter, chilled and diced
225 g - 8 oz Plain flour
1 Egg, beaten
2 tbsp Icing sugar

1. Preheat the oven to 180°C, gas mark 4. Line a 23 cm - 9 inch loose bottom flan tin.

2. To make the pastry, put the flour, icing sugar and butter into the bowl of a food processor and whizz until it resembles fine breadcrumbs. Add the egg and 1 tbsp of cold water and mix again until it starts to bind together. Tip the pastry onto a floured surface, knead together then roll out and line the flan tin. Trim the pastry so that it is a little higher than the dish.

For the Filling:
200 g - 7 oz Honey
75 g - 3 oz Plain chocolate
1 tsp Vanilla extract
75 g - 3 oz Unsalted butter
100 g - 3½ oz Pecan nuts for the filling
2 Eggs medium size
100 g - 3½ oz Pecan halves to decorate
75 g - 3 oz Caster sugar

1. Prepare the filling by breaking the chocolate into small pieces and melt with the butter in a bowl over a pan of simmering water. Cool slightly.

2. In a large bowl, beat together the eggs, sugar, honey, vanilla extract and cooled chocolate. Chop the pecan nuts and fold into the mixture. Pour into the pastry case.

3. Decorate the top with the Pecan halves. Put the tart on a hot baking sheet and bake for 40-45 minutes until just set.

4. Serve warm with cream or ice cream.

Bread And Butter Pudding

This is a very old recipe of which there will be many versions. The following works perfectly with honey. When the pudding is cooked extra honey can be drizzled over the top to enhance the flavour and sweetness.

2 Large slices of thick white bread	1 ½ tbsp Honey
2 tbsp Currants	300 ml - 1/2 pint Milk, full fat
2 tbsp Sultanas	1 tsp Vanilla extract
2 tsp of Chopped mixed peel	½ tsp Cinnamon
2 Eggs plus 1 yolk	1 tbsp Demerara sugar

1. Preheat the oven to 180°C, gas mark 4. Grease a 1 litre - 1¾ pint oven proof dish.

2. Generously butter each slice of bread and cut into quarters. Arrange the bread, buttered side up in the dish. Scatter the currants, sultanas and peel over the top. Drizzle the honey over the dish.

3. Mix together the eggs, yolk and vanilla extract then stir in the milk. Pour the custard carefully over the bread and fruit. Sprinkle with cinnamon and Demerara sugar. Leave to soak for 30 minutes.

4. Put in the oven and cook the pudding for about 40 minutes until the custard is set and the top is brown and crusty. At this point another spoonful of honey can be added to the warm dish if desired.

Old Fashioned Steam Honey Pudding

Makes 4 - 6

2 dsp Honey	75 g - 3 oz Butter
175 g - 6 oz Plain flour	50 g - 2 oz Castor sugar
1 tsp Baking powder	1 Egg
Pinch of salt	Milk to mix

1. Grease a 900 ml - 1½ pint pudding basin.

2. Put one dessert spoon of honey in the bottom of the basin.

3. In a separate bowl sift together the flour, baking powder and salt. Add the sugar then rub in the butter. Beat together the egg and add the other dessert spoon of honey. Stir into the dry ingredients with enough milk to make a dropping consistency. Pour into the pudding basin on top of the honey.

4. Cover with a piece of greased baking paper large enough to tie around the rim of the basin. Steam on a gentle heat 1½ - 2 hours.

5. Turn out onto a serving plate and serve hot with custard.

Pear Tart With Honey And Marzipan

Serves 6

1 x 375 g - 13 oz Pack puff pastry	2 tblsp Honey
50 g - 2 oz Marzipan	1½ tbsp Flaked almonds
2 tbsp Double cream	5 g - 2 oz Plain chocolate
2½ x 410g Tins poached pear halves	

1. Preheat the oven to 220°C, gas mark 7.
Roll out the pastry and line a 20 cm - 8 inch flan dish.

2. Soften the marzipan with the back of a spoon and slowly work the double cream into it to make a paste. Spread the marzipan evenly over the pastry.

3. Arrange the pears on top and scatter with the flaked almonds, then drizzle the honey evenly over the dessert.

4. Bake for about 18 - 20 minutes, until the pastry is risen and golden. Remove from the oven and allow to cool.

5. Melt the chocolate in a bowl over a pan of gently simmering water. Drizzle the chocolate over the cooked tart and serve warm with ice cream.

Baked Apples With Honey And Amaretti Stuffing

This recipe can be made using most varieties of apples, but for preference I would use an eating variety as the skins on these are not quite so tough (Discovery or Empire are ideal).

Serves 4

4 Large unpeeled apples	2 tbsp Sultanas
50 g - 2 oz Amaretti biscuits, crushed	25 g - 1 oz Unsalted butter
1 Orange, zest and juice	2 tbsp Honey

1. Preheat the oven to 190°C, gas mark 5.

2. Remove the cores from the apples. Using a sharp knife score the apples around the middle. Arrange in a shallow heatproof dish.

3. In a bowl mix together the crushed Amaretti biscuits with the sultanas and orange zest and half the juice of the orange.

4. Fill the apples with this mixture. Drizzle over the remaining orange juice and dot each apple with the butter.

5. Bake for 30 minutes remove from oven and drizzle over the honey. Return to the oven for a further 5 - 10 minutes or until tender. Serve with cream or custard.

6. This recipe is for eating apples if a cooking variety is used add a tablespoon of soft brown sugar to the biscuit mixture when filling the apples.

Gooseberry And Honey Flan

This is a good way to use gooseberries when they are plentiful, but any fruit in season, such as rhubarb or plums, can be used. The sharpness of the fruit and their sticky, syrupy juices can be poured over the top of the custard to offset the richness.

This recipe can also be made without using a pastry base. Just make the fruit and custard filling in little ramekins, gently cooked in the oven in a bain-marie.

Serves 6

22 cm - 9 inch Short-crust pastry case	150 g - 5 fl oz Water
225 g - 8 oz Gooseberries	325 ml - 12 fl oz Double cream
60 g - 2 oz Vanilla sugar	75 ml - 3 fl oz Milk, full fat
Slivers of Peel from 1 Orange	1 tbsp Honey
A Knob of Butter	6 Egg yolks

1. Preheat the oven to 190°C, gas mark 5.

2. Bake the pastry blind for 15 minutes then brush with a beaten egg and return to the oven for 5 minutes. Remove the pastry case from the oven and turn the heat down to 180°C, gas mark 4.

3. Stew the fruit gently in a covered saucepan together with the sugar, orange peel, butter and water until softened.

4. Tip the contents of the pan into a sieve over a bowl. Pick out the orange peel and leave until the juice has completely dripped through. Reserve both separately.

5. To make the custard topping, bring the cream, milk and honey to scalding point. If the fruit is very sharp add a little more honey to the mixture. Stir gently then pour in the egg yolks and whisk together.

6. Spread the fruit over the cooled pastry case, then pour over the custard and bake for about 30 minutes, until set.

7. Serve warm, with the juice served separately in a jug.

Honey Cheesecake With Fresh Peaches

Serves 6

| For the Base: | 50 g - 2 oz Butter |
| 175 g - 6 oz Digestive biscuits | 75g - 2 oz Honey |

For the Filling:	50 g - 2 oz Icing sugar
225 g - 8 oz White chocolate	150 ml Double cream
500 g - 18 oz Mascarpone cheese	3 - 4 Fresh peaches depending on size
1 Lemon, juice and zest	Honey for serving

1. A loose bottom flan tin 20 cm - 8 inches.

2. Put the digestive biscuits in a polythene bag and crush with a rolling pin
Melt the butter then mix in the honey and biscuits. Press the mixture firmly into the flan tin.

3. Grate the zest from the lemon and squeeze the juice into a large bowl.
Chop the white chocolate and melt in a bowl over a pan of simmering water. To the chocolate add the mascarpone cheese, lemon zest and juice, and the icing sugar. Mix all these ingredients together thoroughly.

4. Lightly beat the double cream then fold into the mixture. Pour into the prepared base and smooth with a palette knife.

5. Chill in a refrigerator for 30 minuets before removing from the flan tin
Decorate the top with even slices of fresh peaches. Before serving drizzle a little honey over the cheesecake and around the serving dish.

Honey Ginger Puddings

This recipe makes 12 individual puddings

125 g - 4 oz Butter　½ tsp Bicarbonate of soda
120 ml Milk　125 g - 4 oz Brown sugar
125 g - 4 oz Dark honey　1 tbsp Ground ginger
140 g - 5 oz Self-raising flour　2 Eggs
100 g - 3 oz Plain flour

1. Preheat the oven to 180°C, gas mark 4. Grease a 12 hole muffin tin.

2. Put the butter, milk and honey in a small saucepan and stir over a low heat until melted and combined. Do not let the mixture boil. Cool for a few minutes. To the same pan add the sieved flours, bicarbonate of soda, sugar, ginger and eggs. Mix well until smooth.

3. Pour the mixture into the tin filling each hole ¾ full. Bake for 20 - 25 minutes.

4. Cool before removing from the tin. Serve warm with single cream.

Apple And Honey Pudding

This is a very quick and easy pudding which is moist and warming, especially on a cold Autumn day.

Serves 4

150 g - 5 oz Self-raising flour　100 g - 4 oz Honey
75 g - 3 oz Butter　100 g - Sultanas
1 tsp Mixed spice　2 Eggs
2 Large bramley apples

1. Preheat the oven to 180°C, gas mark 4.
Grease a dish about 20.5 cm - 8 inch square.

2. Mix the spice with the flour and rub in the butter to resemble fine breadcrumbs. Prepare the apples: these should be peeled then grated or finely chopped and added to the breadcrumbs, mix well to combine.

3. In a separate bowl beat the eggs and add the honey and sultanas. Add to the mixture and stir well, then pour into the prepared dish.

4. Cook on the middle shelf of the oven for about 35 minutes or until firm to touch.

5. Serve warm with pouring cream.

Pancakes With Honey And Pistachio Syrup

This is a pancake recipe with a difference as the use of yoghurt makes them very light. They can be cooked in advance before a meal and kept warm on a plate covered with a tent of foil in a low oven.

Makes approximately 8

150 g - 6 oz Plain flour	3 tbsp Greek yoghurt
1 tbsp Caster sugar	125 ml Milk
¼ tsp Bicarbonate of soda	1 Large egg
Pinch of ground cardamon	1 tsp Almond oil or a knob of butter, melted
To Serve:	1 - 2 handfuls of shelled and chopped
Orange blossom honey	pistachio nuts

1. Put all the dry ingredients into a large bowl. Spoon the yoghurt into a measuring jug, stirring with a fork, and pour in the milk.

2. Whisk in the egg then the almond oil or butter. Stir this jug of liquid into the bowl of dried ingredients. Almost immediately the mixture will stiffen into a thick fluffy batter.

3. Heat a griddle pan until hot then pour on 2 tbsp of batter, as the mixture is quite thick, spread evenly with the back of a spoon before it sets. When the pancake begins to bubble flip over and cook the other side to golden brown. Keep the pancakes warm under foil as you continue to cook the rest.

4. When ready to serve arrange on a plate and drizzle over a generous amount of honey and sprinkle with the chopped pistachios.

Autumn Crumble With Honey And Chocolate

Crumbles are very popular all the year round, but particularly in the Autumn when there is an abundance of fruit. The following two dishes are a variation on the basic crumble recipe. The use of chocolate adds an interesting twist.

Serves 4

4 Pears, peeled, cored and quartered	50 g - 2 oz Butter
8 Plums, stoned and chopped	60 g - 3 oz Plain flour
2 tbsp Honey	25 g - 1 oz Demerara sugar
25 g - 1 oz Plain chocolate, finely chopped	25 g - Rolled oats

1. Preheat the oven to 180°C, gas mark 4.
Lightly grease a medium size pudding dish, about 1 litre - 1½ pint with butter.

2. Put the pears, plums, honey and chocolate into a bowl and mix well and place into the pudding dish.

3. Make the topping by rubbing together the flour and butter until it resembles fine breadcrumbs. Stir in the sugar and oats. Sprinkle over the fruit mixture and bake for 25 to 30 minutes, until golden and bubbling.

4. Serve with custard or ice cream.

5. The same recipe can be made with 4 eating apples and the appropriate amount of blackberries. If cooking apples are used they should be firm and it may be necessary to add a little more honey to taste.

Rhubarb Tart With Orange And Honey

Wrapping rhubarb in a buttery pastry is the best way to appreciate the flavour and texture of this fruit - like vegetable.

Serves 4 - 6

For the Pastry:
250 g - 9 oz Plain flour
125 g - 4 oz Butter
I Egg yolk
Pinch of salt

1. This quantity of pastry is to fit a tart dish 23 cm - 9 inch. It can be made quickly in a food processor.

2. Sift in the flour and salt into the food processor, then cut the butter into small pieces add to the flour. Process for about 20 - 30 seconds, add the egg yolk, if the pastry is still crumbly add a dash of cold water. The moment it has cohered into a single ball, remove it, wrap in cling film and place in the refrigerator for 30 minutes.

3. Preheat the oven to 190°C, gas mark 5.

For the Filling:
500 g - 1lb 4 oz Rhubarb, trimmed and chopped into 2.3 cm - 1 inch chunk
2 tbsp Cornflour
125 g - 4 oz Sugar
4 tbsp Honey
3 tbsp Orange juice

1. In a large bowl toss the rhubarb with the cornflour then add all the other ingredients. Heat for a minute or two in the microwave until the juice in the rhubarb just starts to run. Leave to stand while you prepare the pastry.

2. Take the pastry from the refrigerator, remove the cling film and divide in half. On a lightly floured working surface roll out the one half of pastry into a circle large enough to line the pie dish with a little overhang. Fill the dish with the rhubarb mixture and about half the juice.

3. Roll out the other half of the pastry in the same way. Brush the edges of the filled dish with a little milk and place the pastry over the top. Crimp the edges with a folk to make a seal. Cut a small hole in the top of the pastry. Brush with a lightly beaten egg or a little milk.

4. Put in the oven for about 40 minutes until golden brown.

5. Serve hot with custard and a small jug of the remaining juice.

Apple And Honey Crumble With Lemon Cheese Sauce

Serves 4 - 6

For the Filling:
5 Medium cooking apples
1 Small piece of fresh ginger
1 tbsp Soft brown sugar
1 tbsp Honey (this amount can vary according to taste)
1 Lemon, juice and peeled rind
Pinch of cinnamon

For the Crumble:
175 g - 6 oz Butter
200 g - 8 oz Plain flour
75 g - 3 oz Demerara sugar
1 tbsp Thick or crystallized honey

For the Sauce:
3 Lemons
100 g - 4 oz Honey
50 g - 2 oz Butter
100 g - 4 oz Soft cream cheese
2 Eggs

1. Preheat the oven to 190°C, gas mark 5.
Grease a large ovenproof pudding dish.

2. Peel and chop the apples into small chunks cook with the juice and rind of the lemon in a pan until just soft. Add the sugar, ginger, honey and cinnamon. Carefully mix together and pour into the prepared dish.

3. In a separate bowl make the crumble by rubbing together the butter, flour, oats and the sugar. Sprinkle on the top of the apple mixture and dot with thick honey. Bake for about 30 minutes until golden brown.

4. To make the sauce gentle beat the eggs, butter, cream cheese and honey. Add the grated zest and juice of the lemons. Place the bowl over a pan of simmering water and whisk gently until the mixture thickens. Take care not to over heat or the sauce will curdle.

5. Serve the pudding hot with the warm sauce.

Walnut And Apple Honey Flan

This flan is a nut lovers dream. It is filled with a dense concoction of nuts, honey and dried fruit.

Serves 6 - 8

For the Pastry:
- 225 g - 8 oz Plain flour
- 2 tbsp Icing sugar
- 124 g - 4 oz Butter, chilled and diced
- 1 Egg beaten

For the Filling:
- 1 tbsp Cherry jam
- 200 g - 7 oz Runny honey
- 125 g - 4 oz Unsalted butter
- 125 g - 4 oz Light muscovado sugar
- 3 Medium eggs
- 1 Lemon, zest and juice
- 125 g - 4 oz Walnuts, roughly chopped
- 125 g - 4 oz Ready-to-eat dried apples and pears, plus 3 dried pears to garnish

1. Preheat the oven to 180°C, gas mark 4. 23 cm - 9 inch loose based flan tin.

2. Put the flour and icing sugar into the bowl of a food processor. Add the butter and mix until the mixture resembles fine breadcrumbs. Add the egg and 1 tbsp of cold water. Pulse until the mixture just starts to come together.

3. Tip pastry onto a work surface and knead gently to form a ball. Wrap in cling film and chill for 20 minutes.

4. To make the filling warm 175 g - 6 oz of the honey in a small pan over a low heat.

5. Put the butter in a large bowl with the sugar. Whisk together until light and fluffy. Add the eggs, lemon zest and juice, walnuts, chopped dried apples and pears, and the warmed honey. Stir well and set aside.

6. Roll out the pastry and ease it into the flan tin. Trim the edges then prick the base with a folk. Place a circle of greaseproof paper in the base and fill with baking beans. Place in the preheated oven and bake for 10 - 15 minutes. Remove the beans then return to the oven for a further 5 minutes until golden.

7. Evenly spread the spoonful of cherry jam over the base of the tart.

Pour in the walnut and honey apple filling and arrange the 3 pears in the centre. Brush with the remaining honey.

8. Put the tart on a baking sheet, cover with foil and bake for 20 minutes. Remove the foil and bake for a further 25 minuets until golden brown and slightly risen.

9. Cool in the tin, then remove, put on a plate and serve with cream or crème fraiche.

Mousses

Here are three delicious mousse recipes. Each one is made using a slightly different method: A chocolate mousse with eggs and cream, a tangy orange using cointreau and a lighter strawberry flavour using tinned fruit. As there is little or no sugar added to tinned fruit these days, the sweetness of honey compliments the mousse perfectly. Any type of berries can be used but strawberry is a favourite.

Tangy Orange Honey Mousse

Serves 6

110 g - 4 oz Dark chocolate	½ Orange, juice and grated zest
3 tbsp Cointreau	290 ml - ½ pint Whipping cream
2 tbsp Honey	2 Egg whites

1. Melt the chocolate with the Cointreau, honey, juice and grated zest of the orange. Leave to cool slightly. Whip the cream and then the egg whites separately to form soft peaks. Fold into the chocolate mixture and spoon into six serving glasses.

2. Chill for 30 minutes.

3. For a decorative finishing touch, melt another 55 g - 2 oz of plain chocolate and using a teaspoon, drizzle zigzags on to a baking parchment. Leave to set, then peel away and decorate the mousse with the chocolate zigzags.

Chocolate Honey Mousse

Serves 4

1 x 200 g - 8 oz Bar of Dark chocolate	300 ml - ½ pint Double cream
1 Egg	Whiskey to taste
1 tbsp Honey	

1. Melt the chocolate slowly over a bowl of warm, not boiling, water.

2. Beat together the egg and honey until pale. Whisk the cream to a soft peak consistency. Add a dash of whiskey and fold in the egg and honey mixture.

3. Pour in the melted chocolate and fold gently until smooth.

4. Spoon into 4 glasses and put in the refrigerator for about an hour before serving.

Strawberry Honey Mousse

Serves 4 - 6

410 g I Tin strawberries : I ½ Block of Jelly
410 g I Tin evaporated milk : 2 tbsp Honey

1. Strain the fruit from the tin into a serving bowl and mash together with the honey. Pour the juice into a measuring jug with the jelly and make up to I ½ pints by adding water if necessary.

2. Melt the jelly, either in a sauce pan over a low heat or in a microwave, then pour all the liquid into the bowl with the fruit and honey. Put in the fridge until the jelly just starts to set. At this point slowly pour in the evaporated milk and gently whisk until the mixture is blended well together.

3. Leave for a few hours to set. Serve with fresh strawberries and cream.

Honey Ice Cream

The following two ice cream recipes are rather special. Both have a luxurious velvety texture and as they are rather rich they should be served in small portions after a main course.

1 Vanilla pod : 250 ml Milk, full fat
500 ml Double cream : 150 ml Set honey

1. Split open the vanilla pod and scrape out the seeds. Put the seeds into a large saucepan with the pod. Pour in the cream and milk and bring them just to a boil. Remove from the heat.

2. Stir in the honey until it dissolves thoroughly. Cover with a lid and leave to cool. When it has cooled remove the vanilla pod and pour the liquid into a bowl, cover with cling film and chill in the fridge for an hour.

3. Then remove and churn in an ice-cream maker or freeze in a shallow container in the freezer, whisking occasionally to break up any ice crystals that might form.

4. Leave for 24 hours before serving.

Luxury Honey Ice Cream

4 Egg yolks : 1 Egg
110 g - 4 oz Honey : 300 ml Double cream
Extra Honey for serving : 25 g - 1 oz Pine nuts toasted

1. Line a 900 g - 2 lb loaf tin with cling film.

2. Whisk the whole egg and the egg yolks with the honey in a bowl over a saucepan of gently simmering water until the mixture is pale and thick. This can be done using a hand-held electric whisk.

3. Whip the double cream until thick, then fold in the egg and honey mixture. Pour into the prepared loaf tin and cover with cling film before putting it in the freezer over night.

4. When it is ready to serve turn out the ice cream onto a suitable sized plate and drizzle with honey, and sprinkle with the toasted pine nuts. This dessert thaws quickly as it stands so serve immediately.

Cake Recipes

From a Welsh Kitchen

Chocolate Batter Cake With Honey And Marzipan Bees

For the Cake:
2 Eggs
225 g - 8 oz Soft butter
200 g - 7 oz Plain flour
200 g - 7 oz Light Muscovado sugar
1 tsp Bicarbonate of soda
125 g - 4 oz Dark chocolate, chopped
1 tbsp Cocoa powder
5 tbsp Honey
200 ml Boiling water

1. Preheat the oven to 180°C, gas mark 4.
Butter and line a 23 cm - 9 inch spring form cake tin.

2. Melt the chocolate in a large bowl over a pan of simmering water. Set aside to cool slightly.

3. Beat the sugar and the butter until soft and creamy, then add the honey.
Beat the eggs gently and add to the mixture with the combined sieved flour and bicarbonate of soda. Mix well. Fold in the melted chocolate and the sieved cocoa powder. Finally add the boiling water. Mix well to a smooth batter and pour into the prepared tin.

4. Cook for 1 hr 30 minutes. After 45 minutes cover the cake lightly with foil checking every 15 minutes.

5. Remove from the oven and let the cake cool completely in the tin before transferring to a wire rack.

For the Honey Glaze:
2 tbsp Honey
200 g - 7 oz Dark chocolate
75 g - 3 oz Icing sugar
60 ml Water

1. To make the glaze heat the water and honey in a saucepan until quite warm. Finely chop the chocolate. Take the liquid off the heat and add the chocolate, mix well and pour in the hot liquid. Add the sieved icing sugar and whisk again until smooth.

2. Remove the cold chocolate honey cake from the tin, pour the icing over and smooth it down the sides.

3. The glaze will remain tacky for about an hour so allow time for it to harden before serving.

4. Do not wash the pan of icing as what is left around the sides can be used for the stripes on the bees.

... Continued

For the Bees: 12 Flaked almonds
25 g - 1 oz Yellow marzipan

1. Divide the marzipan into 6 pieces and roll into bee bodies, slightly tapered at the ends.

2. Using a skewer and the sticky honey glaze left in the pan paint the stripes onto the marzipan - about 3 stripes per bee.

3. Then by using the point of the skewer in the glaze, dot the eyes.

4. Carefully attach the flaked almonds at an appropriate angle to make the wings.

Teisen Lap With Honey

This is sometimes known as a plate cake. Teisen is Welsh for cake and Lap means moist. It is a really quick and easy cake. This traditional cake from Wales would have been packed into the miners lunch boxes and been a great comfort food as they worked deep underground. In the winter years ago it used to be eaten warmed in front of an open fire, these days pop it in the microwave on medium heat for a few seconds.

225 g - 8 oz Self-raising flour : 1 tsp Baking powder
175 g - 6 oz Butter : 1 tsp Mixed spice
3 tbsp Honey : 125 g - 4 oz Sultanas
2 Large eggs :

1. Preheat the oven to 175°C, gas mark 3.
Grease and line a 20 cm - 8 inch round sponge tin.

2. Mix all the dry ingredients together to resemble fine breadcrumbs. This can be done in a food processor. Add the sultanas. Mix together the eggs and honey then pour into the dry ingredients, mix thoroughly to a soft dropping consistency, if necessary add a little milk.

3. Pour into the prepared tin and bake in the oven for 30 - 40 minutes until golden brown and firm to touch.

4. Serve warm or allow to cool on a wire rack.

Family Apple Cake

This mouth-watering cake is packed with fruit. The combination of the apple chunks and honey make an appealing flavour.

75 g - 3 oz Mixed dried fruit	3 Eggs
50 g -2 oz Butter	150 g - 5 oz Plain flour
150 g - 5 oz Caster sugar	¼ tsp Baking powder
50 g - 2 oz Honey	½ tsp Bicarbonate of soda
2 Cooking apples, medium sized	½ tsp Cinnamon
1 tbsp Grated orange rind	100 g - Pecan nuts, chopped
1 tsp Vanilla extract	1 dsp Honey to glaze

1. Preheat the oven to 180°C, gas mark 4.
Grease and line a 20 cm - 8 inch cake tin.

2. Put the dried fruit into a bowl and cover with boiling water. Stand for 5 minutes then drain well.

3. In a saucepan melt the butter, sugar and honey. Peel and chop the apples and add to the saucepan along with the grated orange rind and vanilla extract, then beat the eggs in one at a time.

4. Sift together the flour, bicarbonate of soda and cinnamon into a bowl. Add the dried fruit and pecan nuts, followed by the apple mixture and stir until well combined.

5. Pour into the prepared tin. Bake for 45 to 50 minutes. Cool slightly. Before removing from the tin spoon over the honey to glaze. When further cooled remove from the tin and place on a wire rack.

Honey Almond Cake With Frosting

For the Cake:
125 g - 4 oz Butter
125 g - 4 oz Caster sugar
3 tbsp Honey
3 Eggs
250 g - 10 oz Self-raising flour
Pinch of salt

1½ tsp Ground ginger
1 tsp Mixed spice
1 tsp Cinnamon
100 ml Milk
1 dsp Grated lemon rind
75 g - 3 oz Chopped almonds

1. Preheat the oven to 180°C, gas mark 4. Grease and line a 20 cm - 8 inch cake tin.

2. Cream together the butter honey and castor sugar. Beat in two whole eggs and one yolk, putting aside the one white for the frosting. Add salt and spices to the flour alternatively with the milk. Mix well then add the lemon rind and chopped almonds. Pour into the prepared tin and put into the oven.

3. Cook for 45 to 50 minutes. When cooked remove from the oven and let the cake cool in the tin. Remove from the tin and place on a wire rack while making the topping.

For the Honey Frosting:
1 Egg white (from above)
175 g - 6oz Icing sugar

2 tsp Honey
½ tsp Lemon juice

1. In a bowl whisk the egg whites until stiff, fold in the sieved icing sugar, honey and lemon juice. Place the bowl over a pan of boiling water and continue whisking until thick. Cover the top of the cake and decorate with roasted or flaked almonds.

Tiessennau Mel - Welsh Honey Muffin Cakes

Makes 8

125 g - 4 oz Butter	1 tsp Cinnamon
125 g - 4 oz Brown sugar	½ tsp Baking powder
1 Egg	½ tsp Bicarbonate of powder
4 tbsp Honey	3 tbsp Milk
150 g - 5 oz Plain flour	Demerara sugar, for the topping

1. Preheat the oven to 200°C gas mark 6. Lightly grease a muffin tin with 8 - 10 holes.

2. In a warm bowl cream the butter and sugar until light and fluffy. Separate the egg and beat the yolk and the honey into the creamed mixture. Combine the flour with the cinnamon, baking powder and bicarbonate of soda. Add to the mixture, alternating a little at a time with each table spoon of milk. Whisk the egg white until stiff and fold into the batter mixture.

3. Half fill each muffin tin and sprinkle a little Demerara sugar on top of each one. Bake in the oven for 20 minutes or until light and springy to touch.

4. Remove from the oven, and if desired sprinkle a little more sugar on top. Leave to cool before removing from the tins.

Honey And Apple Slab Cake

This is a very moist cake. While still warm in the tin drizzle another spoonful of honey over the top of the cake, this will add to the flavour and give an attractive glazed effect.

110 g - 4 oz Self-raising flour	75 g - 3 oz Honey
50 g - 2 oz Butter	75 g - 3 oz Sultanas
1 tsp Mixed spice	1 Egg plus 1 Yolk
2 Medium sized Bramley apples	

1. Preheat the oven to 180°C, gas mark 4. Line a shallow cake tin 20 cm - 8 inch square.

2. Place the flour and mixed spice into a bowl and rub in the butter to resemble breadcrumbs. Peel the apples and then grate, or finely chop them into the mixture.

3. Next add the honey, sultanas and eggs and mix together all the ingredients. Pour into the cake tin and bake in the centre of the oven for 30 to 35 minutes.

4. If you wish to add the glaze, drizzle the extra spoonful of honey over the cake whilst still warm in the tin. When the cake is cool remove from the tin and cool in a wire rack.

Honey Orange Slab Cake

This is a quick and easy slab cake to make. It is light and moist with a distinct flavour of honey and orange. The texture is improved if warmed slightly in the microwave before serving. Alternatively a butter cream topping with grated orange can be added for an extra treat if desired.

110 g - 4 oz Butter, softened	2 tsp Orange Peel
4 tbsp Honey	225 g - 8 oz Self-raising flour
2 Eggs	½ tsp Salt
2 tbsp Milk	1 tsp Mixed spice
2 tbsp Fresh orange juice	50 g - 2 oz Sugar

1. Preheat the oven to 180°C, gas mark 4.
Grease and line a 20 cm - 8 inch square baking tray.

2. Cream the butter and the sugar in a large bowl using an electric mixer. Continue creaming while adding the honey in a fine stream. Add the eggs, one at a time, beating well after each addition.

3. Combine milk, orange juice and peel. Sift together the dry ingredients, add to the mixture, beating well after each addition.

4. Pour into the greased tin and bake for 25 - 30 minutes.

5. Remove from the oven and cool in the tin before turning out and cutting into squares.

Honey Carrot Cake

For the Cake:	200 g - 7 oz Wholemeal self-raising flour
120 ml - 4 fl oz Sunflower oil	1 tsp Bicarbonate of soda
2 Eggs	3 tsp Mixed Spice
1 Orange, grated zest	200 g - 7 oz Carrots peeled and grated
200 g - 7 oz Honey	175 g - 6 oz Sultanas

1. Preheat the oven to 170°C, gas mark 3.5.
Use a non-stick baking tin measuring 25.5 x 15 cm -10 x 6 inches, 2.5 cm - 1 inch deep. The base lined with silicone paper.

2. Beat the oil and the eggs together in a bowl. Sift in the flour, bicarbonate of soda and mixed spices. Fold all these ingredients together then stir in the orange zest, grated carrots, sultanas and finally, the honey.

3. Pour into the prepared baking tin and bake for 35 - 40 minutes, until the cake is well risen and springy to touch.

| **For the Honey Glaze:** | 1 dsp Lemon juice |
| 1 dsp Orange juice | 1 tbsp Mild honey |

1. Whilst the cake is baking make the honey glaze by simply mixing together the lemon and orange juice with the honey.

2. Remove the cake from the oven and evenly pierce the surface with a skewer. Quickly pour over the honey glaze.

3. Leave the cake to cool in the tin before removing and cutting into about 12 squares.

Special Honey Sponge Cake

This is a cake that always impresses! It is quick and easy with excellent results.

For the Cake:
250 g - 9 oz Honey
260 g - 10 oz Unsalted butter
3 Large eggs
125 g - 4 oz Muscovado sugar
260 g - 10 oz Self-raising flour

1. Preheat the oven to 160°C or gas mark 3.
Grease a 25 cm - 10 inch loose bottomed cake tin.

2. Cut the butter up into small pieces put in a saucepan with the sugar and honey. Heat gently until it all melts. Slowly increase the heat and let it boil for about a minute. Remove from the heat and let it cool, which takes quite a while.

3. Beat the eggs and add them to the cooled honey mixture ensuring that they are well blended. Sieve the flour into a large mixing bowl, make a well in the middle of the flour and pour in the honey-egg mixture. Stir well.

4. Pour into the prepared cake tin and bake in the moderate oven for 50 minutes or until an inserted skewer comes out clean.

For the Honey Topping:
125 g - 4 oz Icing sugar
125 g - 4 oz Cream cheese
2 tsp Honey

1. Once the cake has cooled you can add the topping. Soften the cream cheese in a bowl then add the sifted icing sugar and honey. Beat together until smooth. If the mixture appears too runny add more icing sugar.

2. Spread with a palette knife on the top of the cooled cake.

Bara Brith

Another family favourite, this Welsh fruit loaf always goes down well with a cup of tea. For a real treat spread a little butter on each slice.

50 g - 2 oz Margarine   120 ml - 4 fl oz Boiling water
225 g - 8 oz Sultanas   225 g - 8 oz Self-raising flour
1 tsp Bicarbonate of soda   1 Egg
1 tsp Mixed Spice   4 tbsp Honey
Pinch of Salt

1. Preheat the oven to 180°C, gas mark 4.
Line a 20 cm x 13 cm or 8 x 5 inch loaf cake tin.

2. Cut the margarine into cubes. Put in a bowl with the sultanas, bicarbonate of soda spices and salt.

3. Pour on the boiling water and mix together until the margarine has melted. Beat in the egg and fold in the flour. Finally add the honey. Mix well.

4. Pour the mixture into the cake tin and bake on the middle shelf of the oven for about one hour. When cooked remove from oven and allow to cool before removing from the tin and placing on a wire rack.

Honey Scones

Scones are very easy to make and by replacing some of the sugar with honey this makes them light and moist.

Makes 8 - 10

250 g - 9 oz Plain flour	25 g - 1 oz Caster sugar
Pinch of salt	2 tbsp Honey
2 tsp Baking powder	1 Egg
1 tsp Cinnamon	75 ml Whole milk
75 g - 3 oz Butter	

1. Preheat the oven to 210°C, gas mark 7.

2. Mix all the dry ingredients together in a bowl. Stir in the sugar and rub in the butter. Add the honey and the beaten egg and mix to a stiff dough. Add the milk.

3. Roll out on a floured board to ½ inch 12 mm in thickness. Cut into rounds with a fluted cutter and brush the tops with milk. Place on a baking tray and put in the oven for 10 to 15 minutes.

4. Cool on a wire rack. Split in half and serve with butter and honey.

5. These scones can also be made from the same recipe using wholemeal flour.

Date And Walnut Cake

225 g - 8 oz Block of dates	1 Egg
Pinch Bicarbonate of soda	2 tbsp Honey
140 ml - ¼ pint Boling tea	225 g - 8 oz Self-raising flour
75 g -3 oz Butter	75 g - 3 oz Chopped walnuts
50 g -2 oz Muscovado sugar	

1. Preheat the oven to 180°C - gas mark 4. Grease and line a 1 kg - 2.2 lb loaf tin.

2. Put the dates in a bowl, add the tea and leave to stand.

3. Meanwhile cream the butter and sugar well. Beat in the egg and honey with one tablespoon of the flour. Sieve the remaining flour into the creamed mixture, fold in along with the nuts, dates and tea.

4. Spoon into the prepared tin. Bake for 1 - 1¼ hours, until golden brown and firm to touch. Remove from the tin and cool on a wire rack.

Date And Nut Honey Squares

Makes 12

75 g - 3 oz Butter	1 tsp Baking powder
6 tbsp Honey	Pinch of salt
3 Eggs	175 g - 6 oz Chopped dates
175 g - 6 oz Plain flour	125 g - 4 oz Chopped mixed nuts

1. Preheat the oven to 180°C, gas mark 4.
Grease a 20 x 30 cms, 8 x 12 inches baking tray.

2. Cream together the butter and honey until light and fluffy. Beat in the eggs one at a time and mix well. Sieve the flour, baking powder and salt together before stirring in. Add the chopped dates and nuts and mix well.

3. Spread the mixture evenly on the greased baking tray. Place in the oven for about 30 minutes until golden brown.

4. Remove from the tin and cool on a wire rack. Cut into squares. They will keep for several weeks in an air tight container.

Honey And Spice Cake With Lemon And Ginger Topping

For the Cake:	Grated zest of 1 small orange
75 g - 3 oz Light runny honey	Grated zest of 1 small lemon
225 g - 8 oz Plain flour	125 g - 4 oz Butter
1 tsp Ground ginger	1 Large egg
1 tsp Ground cinnamon	1 tsp Bicarbonate of soda
Pinch of ground cloves	50 g - 2 oz Chopped candied peel
75 g - 3 oz Caster sugar	

1. Preheat the oven to 170°C, gas mark 3.
Grease and line a 7 inch - 18 cm square tin or and 8 inch - 20 cms round tin.

2. Sieve the flour and spices into a large mixing bowl then add the sugar, the orange and lemon zest. Add the butter in small pieces and rub lightly into the flour until it resembles fine breadcrumbs. Add the beaten egg followed by the honey.

3. Next, in a small basin mix the bicarbonate of soda with 3 tbsp of cold water, stir until dissolved then add to the cake mixture, beat until smooth and soft. Finally, stir in the mixed peel and spoon the mixture into the prepared tin spreading it out evenly. Bake the cake for about 50 minutes until well risen and springy to touch.

4. Cool for 10 minutes before turning out onto a wire rack to finish cooling.

For the Lemon and Ginger Topping:	1 tbsp Lemon juice
175 g - 6 oz Sifted icing sugar	6 Pieces of stem ginger

1. To make the lemon and ginger topping sieve the icing sugar into a bowl add 2 tbsp of warm water along with the lemon juice and mix to a thin consistency add a little more water if necessary. Spread over the top of the cake letting it run down to coat the sides.

2. Decorate the top with the pieces of stem ginger.

Glamorgan Honey Fruit Cake

225 g - 8 oz Self-raising flour	50 g - 2 oz Candied peel
125 g - 4 oz Butter	50 g - 2 oz Glacé cherries
225 g - 8 oz Honey	½ tsp Freshly grated nutmeg
2 Eggs	Pinch of salt
125 g - 4 oz Sultanas	Milk as required
125 g - 4 oz Raisins	

1. Preheat the oven to 175°C, gas mark 4. Grease and line an 20 cm - 8 inch round cake tin, or 20.5 x 12 cm – 8 x 5 inch, oblong tin.

2. Cream the butter and honey together until smooth. Beat the eggs together and add alternately with the sifted flour, salt and nutmeg mixture.

3. Add the dried fruits, peel and cherries. Beat lightly ensuring that the ingredients bind well together. If the mixture is too stiff add a little milk. Pour into the prepared cake tin and bake for about 40 to 50 minutes until well risen and evenly brown.

4. Remove from tin and cool on a wire rack.

Honey Welsh Cakes

A traditional Welsh favourite! The Welsh Cakes when mixed produce a softer texture so use a little more flour when rolling out.

Makes approximately 24

350 g - 12 oz Self-raising flour
175 g - 6 oz Margarine
110 g - 4 oz Sultanas
1 tsp Mixed spice

Pinch of salt
1 Egg plus 1 yoke
150 g - 5 oz Honey

1. Place the flour in a bowl and rub in the margarine, mix until the mixture resembles fine breadcrumbs. Add sultanas, mixed spice and salt.

2. Add the beaten eggs. Finally add the honey and mix to a dough.

3. Roll out to 5 mm - ¼ inch thickness on a well floured board, cut into rounds with a 7.5 cm - 3 inch cutter.

4. Place a griddle or a heavy based frying pan on a moderate heat and grease lightly. Cook the Welsh Cakes for about 3 minutes on each side until golden brown.

5. Leave to cool on a wire rack.

A Special Honey Refrigerator Cake

With no baking involved, this has to be the easiest cake ever. Serve in chunky slices.

Makes about 12

150 g - 5 oz Dried apricots	125 g - 4 fl oz Brandy
150 g - 5 oz Ready-to-eat prunes	350 g - 12 oz Plain chocolate
3 Large balls of stem ginger	150 g - 5 oz Unsalted butter
1 tbsp Syrup from the jar of stem ginger	175 g - 6 oz Digestive biscuits, crushed
3 tbsp Honey	

1. Lightly oil a tin that measures 18 x 18 cm - 7 x 7 inches, then line it with cling film, leaving enough hanging over the rim to wrap the cake entirely.

2. Chop the apricots, prunes and stem ginger. Put into a pan with the ginger syrup, honey and brandy. Gently simmer for 2 - 3 minutes. Remove from the heat and leave the fruit to soak in the syrup for 30 minutes.

3. Meanwhile, break up the chocolate and put in a large bowl with the butter. Place the bowl over a pan of gently simmering water. Stir slowly until the butter and chocolate have melted. Add the crushed biscuits and the soaked fruit to the mixture combining it all together.

4. Spoon the cake mixture into the prepared tin and level the surface. Seal up in the cling-film and chill for at least 6 hours or over night.

Biscuit Recipes

From a Welsh Kitchen

Country Nut Biscuits

Makes 20

125 g – 4 oz Butter : 100 g - 3½ oz Rolled oats
100 g - 3½ oz Light brown sugar : 1 tsp Cinnamon
50 g – 2 oz Honey : 75 g - 3 oz Chocolate chips
140 g - 4½ oz Plain flour : 75 g - 3 oz Chopped walnuts
1 Egg :

1. Preheat the oven to 170°C, gas mark 3. Lightly grease two large baking trays.

2. In a large bowl cream together the butter, sugar and honey until light and fluffy. Add the egg then mix in all the dry ingredients. Stir until well combined.

3. Put large tablespoonfuls of the mixture on the prepared baking trays, spacing them well apart.

4. Bake for 12 - 15 minutes until golden. When cooked carefully lift the biscuits off the tray and leave to cool on a wire rack.

5. For a special occasion drizzle some melted chocolate over the top.
Store in an airtight container.

Honey Walnut Biscuits

Makes 12 -14

175 g - 6 oz Butter : 125 g - 4 oz Chopped walnuts
175 g - 6 oz Caster sugar : 225 g - 9 oz Plain flour
1 Egg : 2 tsp Baking powder
3 tbsp Honey :

1. Preheat the oven to 180°C, gas mark 4. Grease a large baking tray.

2. Cream the butter and sugar until light and fluffy. Add the egg, honey and walnuts. Sieve the flour and baking powder together and combine with the creamed mixture.

3. Put small spoonfuls of the mixture on to the well buttered baking tray, placing the drops well apart, allowing them room to spread.

4. Bake for approximately 15 minutes. When cooked carefully lift the biscuits off the tray and leave to cool on a wire rack.

Chocolate And Honey Refrigerator Slices

The combination of honey and chocolate makes a very smooth and delicious chocolate slice. These can be as simple or sophisticated as you wish to make them. The marshmallows and cherries can be replaced with nuts, (macadamia are excellent) and any other fruit such as dried figs, apricots or raisins.

Makes 16

25 g - 1 oz Unsalted butter	100 g - 3½ oz Digestive biscuits
3 tbsp Honey	100 g - 3½ oz Marshmallows
300 g - 11 oz Dark chocolate	100 g - 3½ oz Glace cherries
100 g - 3½ oz Milk chocolate	Cocoa powder for dusting

1. Lightly grease a 18cm - 7 inch square baking tray.

2. Break up the dark and milk chocolate into pieces. Put the butter, honey and both types of chocolate into a saucepan and melt over a low heat. Stir gently from time to time. Meanwhile roughly break the biscuits and then chop the marshmallows and the cherries. Stir all these into the melted chocolate mixture.

3. Tip the mixture into the prepared tin. Refrigerate for 2-3 hours or until firmly set. Cut into 16 slices and dust with cocoa powder.

Muesli Bars With Honey

Makes 12

50 g - 2 oz Butter softened
3 tbsp Honey
150 g - 5 oz Rolled oats
75 g - 3 oz Sultanas
75 g - 3 oz Walnuts or chopped nuts

75 g - 3 oz Fruit muesli
50 g - 2 oz Pumpkin seeds
50 g - 2 oz Sunflower seeds
1 Dessert apple
100 ml - 3½ fl oz Apple juice

1. Preheat the oven to 200°C, gas mark 6. Lightly grease a 25cm - 8 inch square baking tray.

2. Melt the butter and honey in a pan, stir in the oats, sultanas, nuts, fruit muesli and the seeds. Combine these ingredients well together. Grate the apple and add the apple juice to the mixture. Stir well, then pour into the prepared tin and level.

3. Place in the oven and bake for 25 - 30 minutes until golden brown.

4. Mark into squares while still warm. Leave to cool before cutting and serving.

Oat And Sultana Honey Biscuits

Makes 12- 14

125 g - 4 oz Unsalted butter
75 g - 3 oz Light muscovado sugar
1 Egg
50 g - 2 oz Self-raising flour
150 g - 5 oz Rolled oats

¼ tsp - Baking powder
Grated zest of 1 lemon
50 g - 2 oz Sultanas
1 tbsp - Honey

1. Preheat the oven to 190°C or gas mark 5. Grease two baking sheets with butter.

2. In a large bowl cream together the butter and sugar until pale and fluffy. Beat in the egg until combined. Stir in the flour, rolled oats, baking powder, lemon zest, sultanas and honey.

3. Dust a working surface with a little of the flour, then take pieces of the mixture and roll into 12 even sized balls. Place them on the greased baking sheets spaced well apart. Flatten them with your fingers.

4. Bake for 12 - 15 minutes until golden. When cooked carefully lift the biscuits off the tray and leave to cool on a wire rack.

5. Store in an air-tight tin and these biscuits are best eaten within a week.

Honey Coffee Kisses

This and the next recipe " Honey Fingers" are unusual in that they require the use of crystallised honey.

Makes 12

175 g - 6 oz Self-raising flour	75 g - 3 oz Butter
Pinch of salt	1 Egg
75 g - 3 oz Sugar	1 tbsp strong coffee e.g cold expresso
For the filling:	1 tsp Strong coffee e.g cold expresso
50 g - 2oz Icing sugar	Crystallised honey
25 g - 1oz Butter	

1. Preheat the oven to 180°C, gas mark 4. Grease a large baking tray.

2. Rub the butter into the flour, sugar and salt to resemble breadcrumbs. Beat the egg and stir in with the coffee. Mix all ingredients together to make a firm dough.

3. Form into about 24 small balls. Place on a greased baking tray and bake for 15 to 20 minutes.

4. Prepare the filling by mixing all the ingredients, except the honey, together. When the biscuits are cold take half of the quantity and place a knob of crystallised honey in the centre of each biscuit and surround it with the filling and sandwich the biscuits together in pairs.

Honey Oat Chocolate Flapjacks

This recipe, sometimes known as flapjacks, was given to me by my daughter and has become a firm family favourite. It is ideal for an 'energy boost' when travelling or walking.

Makes 18

155 g - 5½ oz Rolled oats	175 g - 6 oz Sultanas
155 g - 5½ oz Plain flour	175 g - 6 oz Chocolate chips
175 g - 6 oz Castor sugar	175 g - 7 oz Melted butter
175 g - 6 oz Chopped pecan nuts or walnuts	4 tbsp Set honey

1. Preheat the oven to 180°C, gas mark 4.
Lightly grease a 20 x 30 cms, 8 x 12 inches, baking tray.

2. Combine the oats, sifted flour, sugar, nuts, sultanas and chocolate chips in a large bowl. Stir in the melted butter and honey. Mix well.

3. Press the mixture evenly into the prepared tin, bake in the moderate oven for about 25 minutes or until lightly browned. Cool on a wire rack and mark into slices in the pan before cutting.

Honey Nut Biscuits

Treat your friends at a coffee morning with these delicious chocolate, honey and nut biscuits.
Makes 20

25 g - 1 oz Plain chocolate • 50 g - 2 oz Caster sugar
25 g - 1 oz Butter • 75 g - 3 oz Plain flour
1 tbsp Thick honey • 50 g - 2 oz Walnuts finely chopped
1 Egg beaten

1. Preheat the oven to 180°C, gas mark 4. Grease three baking sheets.

2. Break the chocolate into small pieces and place in a basin, together with the butter and honey. Stand it over a pan of simmering water until the chocolate and butter have melted. Remove from the heat and leave to cool slightly, before stirring in the remaining ingredients.

3. Drop the mixture in teaspoonfuls onto the baking sheets, leaving room for them to spread.

4. Bake for 12 to 15 minutes until the biscuits have risen slightly and are firm. Leave to cool for 1 minute, then lift off and leave on a wire rack to cool completely. Store in an airtight container.

Chocolate Honey Krispies

Makes 12

175 g - 6 oz Milk or dark chocolate • 175 g - 6 oz Rice krispies
2 dtsp Set honey • 50 g - 2 oz Raisins
75 g - 3 oz Butter • 50 g - 2 oz Cherries, chopped

1. Grease and line a 20.5 cm - 8 inch square baking tray with baking parchment making sure it comes over the edges of the tray.

2. Melt the chocolate in a bowl over a pan of simmering water. Spread as a base in the lined baking tray.

3. Melt the butter and mix with the honey. Stir in the rice krispies, raisins and cherries, combine well and spread on top of the chocolate base. This should still be just soft so the two layers stick together.

4. Place in the refrigerator for a few hours until firm enough to cut into chunky pieces.

Bran And Honey Bars

Makes 12 - 14

150 g - 5 oz Butter	Butter Cream Ingredients:
6 tbsp Set honey	125 g - 4 oz Butter
2 Eggs	2 tbsp Set honey
50 g - 2 oz Self-raising flour	1 tbsp Milk
175 g – 6 oz Plain flour	175 g - 6 oz Icing sugar
75 g - 3 oz All Bran	
3 tbsp Oil, preferably corn oil	

1. Preheat the oven to 180°C, gas mark 4.
Grease a 20 x 30 cms, 8 x 12 inches baking tray. Line with enough baking paper to allow the finished bars to be lifted clear of the tray.

2. Beat the butter and honey in a small bowl with an electric mixer until smooth. Add the eggs, one at a time, and beat until combined. Stir in the sifted flours, bran and oil. Spread the mixture in the prepared tin and bake in the oven for about 25 minutes or until well browned.

3. Lift carefully from the tray and rest on a wire rack to cool.

4. To make the butter cream, beat the butter in a bowl with an electric mixer until light and fluffy. Add the honey and milk and beat until combined. Gradually stir in the icing sugar, spread over the cooled biscuit and cut into bars.

Honey Fingers

Makes 12

175 g - 6 oz Butter	1 Egg
275 g - 10 oz Plain flour	Crystallised honey
125g - 4 oz Soft brown sugar	Icing sugar for dusting

1. Preheat the oven to 175°C, gas mark 4.

2. Rub the butter into the flour to resemble breadcrumbs, stir in the sugar, beat the egg and add to the mixture to make a stiff dough. Divide into half and roll into 2 equal oblongs. Mark each oblong into twelve fingers. Place on the baking tray and prick with a fork.

3. Place in the oven for 25 minutes. When cooked allow to cool before cutting along the marks into 24 fingers. Spread 12 pieces with the crystallised honey and sandwich with the other 12. Dust with icing sugar.

Honey Shortbread Biscuits

Makes 12

50 g - 2 oz Honey ⁞ 225 g - 8 oz Butter
50 g - 2 oz Light soft brown sugar ⁞ 400 g -14 oz Plain flour

1. Preheat the oven to 160°C, gas mark 2. Grease a large baking tray.

2. Cream the butter and sugar together, add the honey and gradually add the sifted flour. Mix well together to form a soft dough.

3. Roll out the dough an a lightly floured surface and cut into shapes, prick with a fork and place on a greased baking tray before placing in the oven and bake for about 25 minutes or until the biscuits are golden brown.

4. When cooked carefully lift the biscuits off the tray and leave to cool on a wire rack.

Chocolate Chip Biscuits

Makes 14

175 g - 6 oz Honey	Pinch of salt
125 g - 4 oz Butter	½ tsp Vanilla extract
1 Small egg	125 g - 4 oz Chocolate chips
175g - 6 oz Self-raising flour	50 g - 2 oz Chopped nuts

1. Preheat the oven to 180°C, gas mark 4. Grease a large baking tray.

2. Cream the butter and honey until light and fluffy. Add the egg and mix well. Sift the flour and salt and add to the mixture. Add the vanilla extract, fold in the chocolate and nuts.

3. Using a teaspoon drop the mixture onto the baking tray allowing room for them to spread.

4. Place in the oven for 12 to 15 minutes. When cooked, cool on a wire rack.

Christmas Recipes

From a Welsh Kitchen

Special Honey Christmas Cake

450 g - 16 oz Sultanas
250 g - 9 oz Raisins
125 g - 4 oz Mixed peel
125 g - 4 oz Glace cherries
125 g - 4 oz Stem ginger
8 tbsp Dark rum
250 g - 9 oz Butter
10 tbsp Honey

1 tsp Vanilla extract
4 Large eggs
250 g - 9 oz Dark chocolate
250 g - 9 oz Plain flour
125 g - 4 oz Chopped walnuts
1 tsp Cinnamon
1 tsp Ground nutmeg

1. Chop the cherries and ginger and put all the dried fruit in a large bowl pour in the rum and allow to stand for several hours, or preferably over night.

2. Preheat the oven to 140°C, gas mark 1.
Prepare a deep 20 cm - 8 inch round or square cake tin by lining it with baking paper and wrap brown paper around the outside of the tin.

3. Beat together the butter and honey until light and creamy, add the vanilla extract. Melt the chocolate over a pan of simmering water then add to the butter and honey mixture. Add the spices to the flour. Beat the eggs then gradually fold the sifted flour and eggs into the rest of the mixture. Add the walnuts and prepared fruit. Give everything a good stir to thoroughly combine.

4. Pour into the prepared cake tin. Place a piece of brown paper on top having cut a small hole in the centre about the size of a 50 pence piece.

5. Place in the centre of the oven for about 4 hours. Do not open the oven during the first 3 hours of cooking. Test with a skewer. When the cake is done remove from the oven and allow to cool in the tin.

6. Wrap in grease proof paper and store in an air tight tin until you are ready to decorate.

Ginger And Honey Glazed Ham

Serves 8 - 10

5.4 kg or 12 lb Unsmoked gammon joint
2 Shallots or onions peeled and quartered
6 Cloves
3 Bay leaves
A few sprigs of thyme

2 Carrots cut into chunks
2 Celery sticks cut into chunks
5 cm - 2 inch piece of Root ginger
2 tbsp Honey
2 tbsp Dijon mustard

1. Preheat the oven to 200°C, gas mark 6.

2. Put the gammon into a large saucepan. Add the shallots, cloves, bay leave, thyme, carrots celery sticks and enough cold water to cover. Bring to the boil, then cover and simmer gently on a low heat for 5 hours.

3. Remove any scum with a slotted spoon. Discard the herbs and vegetables and leave the ham to cool in the poaching liquid; this will keep it succulent.

4. When cool, using a sharp knife carefully cut away the thick skin to leave an even layer of fat. Score a diamond pattern in the fat. Put the gammon on a lightly oiled roasting tray. Peel and slice the ginger then evenly tuck into the fat. Mix the honey and mustard together and brush over the gammon.

5. Cook in the oven for 30 - 40 minutes, or until the fat is crisp and caramelised. When cooked allow to cool completely before carving.

Cranberry, Honey And Ginger Sauce

This is the perfect sauce for serving with all meats at Christmas but especially with cold turkey or ham.

Serves 8

2 Large oranges
350 g - 12 oz Cranberries
4 tbsp Runny honey

150 g - ¼ pint Red wine
2.5 cm - 1 inch Root ginger

1. Remove the zest from the oranges and place in a pan, and then squeeze the juice of the oranges into the pan. Finely grate the ginger and add to the pan along with the cranberries, honey and wine. Bring to the boil, then simmer gently uncovered for about 25 minutes. Using a slatted spoon remove half the cranberries and put them into a blender. Whiz until smooth, then return the puree to the pan and mix well. Taste the sauce and add extra honey if necessary. Spoon into a bowl and serve.

2. This can be stored in the fridge in a sealed jar for several days.

Sticky Honey Sausages

Serves 12

900 g - 2 lb Chunky herb sausages : 5 tbsp Hoisin sauce
3 tbsp Runny honey : 1 tsp White mustard

1. Preheat the oven to 200°C, gas mark 6.

2. Place the honey, hoisin sauce and mustard in to a bowl.
Divide the sausage into two by twisting in the middle and snipping.
Toss in the honey mixture.

3. Cook in a roasting tin for 35 - 40 minutes, stirring occasionally.

Parsnips With A Mustard And Honey Glaze

Oven roasted vegetables are very popular at this time of the year and the use of honey really enhances the flavour. People who normally don't like certain vegetables will enjoy them when cooked this way with honey

1.35 kg - 3 lb Parsnips : 2 tbsp Whole grain mustard
3 tbsp Ground nut oil : 2 tbsp Honey
Freshly milled salt and pepper :

1. Preheat the oven to 140°C, gas mark 1.
Place a baking tray containing the ground nut oil on the top shelf of the oven
to preheat.

2. Peel and top and tail the parsnips. Cut them in half through the centre. Cut the top half into 4 and the bottom half into 2 so that you have even sized pieces. Cut out any woody stems from the centre. Par boil the parsnips in a little salted water for about 5 minutes.

3. Drain the parsnips and pat with kitchen roll to remove surplus water. Remove the baking tray and add the parsnips rounded side up to the sizzling oil. Baste the parsnips to make sure they are covered with the oil. Give them a good grinding of pepper and return the tray to the oven. Bake for about 25 minutes, by this time they should be browned and crispy.

4. Meanwhile make the glaze. Mix the mustard and honey together in a bowl, and then using a brush coat the parsnip pieces liberally. Return to the oven for about 8 minutes. Serve immediately.

Spiced Red Cabbage With Honey

Serves 8

25 g - 1 oz Butter
3 Red onions, finely chopped
900 g - 2 lb Red cabbage, shredded
2 Bramley cooking apples
3 tbsp Honey

5 tbsp Red wine vinegar
1 Cinnamon stick
1 Whole clove
2 Thyme sprigs

1. Preheat the oven to 170°C, gas mark 3.

2. Melt the butter in a large flameproof casserole dish. Fry the onions for 7 - 10 minutes until they begin to soften. Peel, core and slice the apples, then add these with the rest of the ingredients and stir together. Season well.

3. Cover the casserole and cook in the oven for 2 hours, stirring once or twice during cooking.

4. Remove from the oven and discard the thyme, cinnamon stick and clove, before placing into a serving dish.

5. This is a recipe that can be made well in advance and frozen for a few months.

Orange And Lemon Carrots With Honey

Serves 8

900 g - 2 lbs Carrots	50 g - 2 oz Butter
150 ml - ¼ pint Orange juice	2 tbsp Honey
150 ml - ¼ Dry white wine	4 tbsp Fresh coriander
2 Lemons	

1. Cut the carrots into long batons, put into a pan with the orange juice, white wine and the squeezed juice of the 2 lemons. Add the butter and honey, place a lid on the pan and bring to the boil. Remove the lid then boil vigorously until the carrots are tender and most of the liquid has evaporated. This will take about 10 minutes.

2. Roughly chop the coriander and sprinkle over the carrots when ready to serve.

Honey Glazed Carrots And Shallots

Chantenay carrots are very good for this recipe. They are extra sweet and look very attractive when served. You can use normal carrots if you prefer.

Serves 8

24 Shallots, peeled, trimmed and left whole	40 g - 1½ oz Butter
500 g -1 lb 2 oz Chantenay carrots	Chopped fresh parsley to garnish
1 tbsp Runny honey	

1. Put the shallots and carrots in a large shallow pan with enough water to come halfway up the vegetables. Lightly salt the water. Cover and simmer rapidly for 5 - 10 minutes until almost tender.

2. Uncover, simmer the liquid rapidly until almost evaporated, then stir in the honey and butter. Continue cooking and stirring for 2 minutes until the vegetables are tender and coated with the glaze. Garnish with the parsley and serve.

Honey Seeded Roasted Roots

3 tbsp Goose fat	2 tbsp Honey
700 g - 1½ lb Parsnips, carrots and swede	1 tbsp Sesame seeds
Salt and pepper	Chives, finely chopped

1. Preheat the oven to 200°C, gas mark 6.

2. Put the goose fat into a roasting tin large enough to hold the vegetables in one layer. Chop all the vegetables in half or quartered depending on their size. Put the roasting tin in the oven to heat.

3. When the goose fat is very hot add the vegetables and season. Toss the vegetables in the fat and cook for 30 - 40 minutes until they are tender and turning brown at the edges.

4. In a small bowl, mix together the honey and sesame seeds. When the vegetables are almost cooked, tip away any excess fat and add the honey mixture. Cook for another 5 - 10 minutes until they are sticky and cooked through. Sprinkle with the chopped chives and some extra sesame seeds to garnish. Serve immediately.

Honey Mince Pies

Makes About 12

225 g - 8 oz Plain flour	1 tbsp Honey
125 g - 4 oz Butter, cut into small pieces	1 Small egg
Pinch of salt	Prepared mincemeat

1. Preheat the oven to 180°C, gas mark 4.

2. Make the pastry by sifting the flour and salt together, add the butter and mix by hand, or in a food processor, until like fine bread crumbs. Mix together the egg and honey. Combine all the ingredients to make into a stiff dough.

3. Roll out and cut into circles to line about 12 pies in a patty tin. Fill with mincemeat. Brush the edges with a little milk then cut smaller circles to fit on top. Nip the edges to close together and brush the tops with beaten egg or milk.

4. Place in the oven and bake for about 20 - 25 minutes. Remove and cool on a wire rack.

Brandy Butter With Honey

This is a great dish to have in the fridge over Christmas; it goes with everything from Christmas pudding and mince pies, to hot tea cakes and a fruit tart. Adding light brown sugar and honey instead of the usual icing sugar gives a lovely caramelised flavour.

225 g - 8 oz Unsalted butter

50 g - 2 oz Soft light brown sugar

2 dsp Honey

3 tbsp Brandy

A squeeze of lemon juice

2 tbsp Clotted cream

Nutmeg to taste

Zest of ½ orange to serve

1. Remove the butter from fridge before starting this recipe so that it is at room temperature. Put the butter in a large bowl and beat with an electric beater or wooden spoon until soft. Gradually add the sugar and honey. At this stage it may be easier to use your hands. Slowly drizzle in the brandy and lemon juice and incorporate in the same way being careful not to go too fast or the mixture will separate. Mix in the clotted cream. Grate over the nutmeg to taste, then store in the fridge.

2. Top with the orange zest before serving.

Honey Cranberry Biscotti

These Italian style biscuits are delicious served with a glass of port or as an accompaniment to honey ice cream. Recipes for ice cream can be found in the dessert section.

Makes approximately 24

110 g - 4½ oz Butter at room temperature
250 g - 9 oz Set honey
2 Eggs
1 tsp Vanilla extract
380 g - 14 oz Plain flour
2 tsp Baking powder

½ tsp Salt
¼ tsp Bicarbonate of soda
2 tsp Cinnamon
100 g - 3½ oz Dried cranberries
50 g - 2 oz Flaked almonds

1. Preheat the oven to 180°C, gas mark 4.

2. Grease and line a baking sheet.

3. Using an electric mixer beat together the butter and honey until creamy. Gradually add the eggs and vanilla extract, beating until smooth.

4. In another bowl, mix together the flour, spices, salt, baking powder and bicarbonate of soda and then gradually add to the honey mixture combining well together. Stir in the cranberries and almonds.

5. Tip the dough onto a well floured surface. Halve the mixture and roll into two evenly shaped oblongs about an inch thick. Place on the baking sheet and bake for 15 minutes or until light golden brown.

6. Remove from the oven and cool for 5 minutes. Turn the oven down to a medium heat. Transfer the logs to a cutting board and cut each log into ½ inch rings. Return to the baking sheet and bake for another 10 - 15 minutes or until crisp. Cool on a wire rack.

Honey Fruit Fingers

The mincemeat filling in these fingers gives them a lovely flavour. The mixture can also be cut into larger pieces and served as a pudding with custard.

Makes about 10 fingers.

100 g - 4 oz Plain flour
1 tsp Baking powder
75 g - 3 oz Butter
50 g - 2 oz Caster sugar

75 g - 3 oz Rolled oats
2 tbsp Honey
4 tbsp Mincemeat

1. Preheat the oven to 180°C, gas mark 4.
Grease a 17.5cm - 7 inch square baking tray.

2. Place all the ingredients in a bowl, except for the mincemeat, and mix well to form a dough. Turn on to a lightly floured board, knead until smooth and divide the mixture in half.

3. Roll out one half and place it in the tin, then cover it with mincemeat. Press down lightly. Roll out the other half and place over the mincemeat.

4. Bake in the oven for about 30 - 40 minutes until golden brown. Leave to cool in the tin for 20 minutes, then score into fingers and set aside to cool completely. When cold gently remove from the tin.

Mulled Cider With Honey

Mulled drinks are always popular at this time of the year so instead of the usual mulled wine, why not try mulled cider as an interesting alternative. As we have large quantities of home made cider this is a personal recipe much enjoyed by the family.

The quantity of these ingredients varies with personal taste so it is best to experiment with what suits each individual. This is just a guide:

750 ml Cider	I Star anise
3 Oranges	2 dsp Brown sugar
I Cinnamon stick	5 dsp Strong flavoured Honey e.g. heather
6 Cloves	200 ml Ginger wine
I Vanilla pod	

1. Pour the cider into a large saucepan. Add all the spices and slit open the vanilla pod and drop it, pod and seeds, into the cider. Save some of the cloves to stud an orange. Next add some honey. Heather honey is very good as it has a strong treacly flavour. Add the brown sugar to taste then cut up some oranges and stir them in also the whole orange studded with the cloves. Add the ginger wine, depending on your taste, this will give the cider a spicy edge and finally add the star anise.

2. Keep it on a hot heat until it tastes just right. Don't allow it to boil as this burns off the alcohol.

Index

Index

Chicken	Autumn salad with chicken and a spicy pumpkin and honey dressing 42	Chocolate	Chocolate chip 90

Chicken

Autumn salad with chicken and a spicy pumpkin and honey dressing 42
Chicken marinated in honey and mead 18
Chicken thighs with lemon honey and potato wedges 13
Chicken with ginger and honey 9
Chicken with honey lemon sauce 19
Honey chicken and noodle stir-fry 15
Oriental honeyed pork or chicken 20
Soy honey chicken with sesame spinach 7
St David's Day chicken with honeyed leeks 21
Warm winter salad with honey and vegetables 44

Chilli

Autumn salad with chicken and a spicy pumpkin and honey dressing 42
Baked sea bass with honey and lemongrass 24
Cod with coconut and honey 25
Honey chicken and noodle stir fry 15
Soy honey chicken with sesame spinach 7
Spicy beef medallions with sesame honey 6

Chives

Honey roast corn on the cob 36
Honey seeded roots 97
Leek terrine with honey and mustard vinaigrette 39
Mackerel with honey and herb stuffing 28
Salmon with dill and honey sauce 31

Chocolate

A special honey refrigerator cake 79
Autumn crumble with honey and chocolate 55
Chocolate and honey Pecan tart 47
Chocolate and honey refrigerator slice 83
Chocolate batter cake with honey and marzipan bees 64

Chocolate

Chocolate chip 90
Chocolate honey Krispies 87
Chocolate honey mousse 59
Country nut biscuits 82
Honey cheesecake with fresh peaches 52
Honey nut biscuits 87
Honey oat chocolate flapjacks 86
Pear tart with honey and marzipan 49
Special honey Christmas cake 92
Tangy orange honey mousse 59

Cider

Mulled cider with honey 102

Cinnamon

Apple and honey crumble with lemon cheese sauce 57
Bread and butter pudding 48
Country nut biscuits 82
Crispy duck with honey and mead 17
Family apple cake 67
Honey and almond cake with honey frosting 68
Honey and spice cake with lemon and ginger topping 76
Honey cranberry biscotti 100
Honey Scones 74
Mulled cider with honey 102
Special honey Christmas cake 92
Spiced red cabbage with honey 95
Tiessennau – Welsh honey muffin cakes 69

Clotted Cream

Brandy butter with honey 99

Cloves

Ginger and honey glazed ham 93
Honey and spice cake with lemon and ginger topping 76
Mulled cider with honey 102
Spiced red cabbage with honey 95

Cocoa

Chocolate batter cake with honey and marzipan bees 64
Chocolate and Honey refrigerator slice 83

Coconut

Cod with coconut and honey 25

Garlic	Honey roast squash with vegetables and couscous 38	Haddock	Haddock with honey and soy dressing 30
	Honeyed lamb and vegetable stir-fry 14	Hoisin Sauce	Sticky honey sausage 94
	Lamb shanks with honey 12		
	Oriental honeyed pork or chicken 20	Jelly	Strawberry mousse 60
	Pork spare ribs with honey and garlic 10	Lamb	Honeyed lamb and vegetable stir-fry 14
	Soy honey chicken with sesame spinach 7		Lamb Shanks with honey 12
	Spicy beef medallions with sesame honey 6		Welsh lamb with orange and honey 8
	Welsh lamb with orange and honey 8	Leeks	Leek terrine with honey and mustard vinaigrette 39
			St David's Day chicken with honeyed leeks 21
Ginger	Apple and honey crumble with lemon cheese sauce 57		
	Baked sea bass with honey and lemongrass 24	Lemon	Apple and honey crumble with lemon cheese sauce 57
	Chicken with ginger and honey 9		Autumn salad with chicken and a spicy pumpkin and honey dressing 42
	Chicken with honey lemon sauce 19		Brandy butter with honey 99
	Cranberry honey and ginger sauce 93		Chicken marinated in honey and mead 18
	Crispy duck with honey and mead 17		Chicken thighs with lemon honey and potato wedges 13
	Ginger and honey glazed ham 93		Chicken with honey lemon sauce 19
	Ginger and turkey meatballs with honey sauce 16		Ginger and turkey meatballs with honey sauce 16
	Honey and almond cake with honey frosting 68		Honey and almond cake with honey frosting 68
	Honey and mandarin swordfish 29		Honey and spice cake with lemon and ginger topping 76
	Honey and spice cake with lemon and ginger topping 76		Honey carrot cake 71
	Honey chicken and noodle stir-fry 15		Honey cheesecake with fresh peaches 52
	Honey ginger puddings 53		Honey chicken and noodle stir-fry 15
	Pork spare ribs with honey and garlic 10		Mackerel with honey and herb stuffing 28
	Soy honey chicken with sesame spinach 7		Oat and sultana honey biscuits 84
			Orange and lemon carrots with honey 96
Ginger Wine	Mulled cider with honey 102		Pork spare ribs with honey and garlic 10
			Roast loin of pork with special honey apple sauce 11
Gooseberries	Gooseberry and honey tart 51		Salmon fillet baked with lemon and honey 26
Greek yogurt	Pancakes with honey and pistachio syrup 54		Salmon with dill and honey sauce 31
	Salmon with dill and honey sauce 31		

Nuts	Honey chicken and noodle stir-fry 15	Onions	Warm winter salad with honey and vegetables 44
	Honey cranberry biscotti 100		Welsh lamb with orange and honey 8
	Honey nut biscuits 87		Winter salad with turkey and a honey and mustard vinaigrette 43
	Honey oat chocolate flapjacks 86		
	Honey roast squash with vegetables and couscous 38		
	Honey walnut biscuits 82	Orange	Baked apple with honey and Amaretti stuffing 50
	Luxury honey ice cream 61		Brandy butter with honey 99
	Muesli bars with honey 84		Cranberry honey and ginger sauce 93
	Pancakes with honey and pistachio syrup 54		Crispy duck with honey and mead 17
	Pear tart with honey and marzipan 49		Family apple cake 67
	Special honey Christmas cake 92		Gooseberry and honey tart 51
	Spring salad with honey and caramelised walnuts 40		Honey and spice cake with lemon and ginger topping 76
	Walnut and apple flan 58		Honey carrot cake 71
			Honey orange slab cake 70
Nutmeg	Autumn flan with honey cheese and nuts 34		Lamb shanks with honey 12
	Brandy butter with honey 99		Mulled cider with honey 102
	Glamorgan honey fruit cake 77		Orange and lemon carrots with honey 96
	Special Honey Christmas cake 92		Rhubarb tart with orange and honey 56
	St. David's Day chicken with honeyed leeks 21		Roast loin of pork with special honey apple sauce 11
			Sauce for salmon 32
Olives	Autumn salad with chicken and a spicy pumpkin and honey dressing 42		Spring salad with honey and caramelised walnuts 40
			Tangy orange honey mousse 59
			Welsh lamb with orange and honey 8
Onions	Autumn flan with honey cheese and nuts 34		
	Chicken thighs with lemon honey and potato wedges 13	Oregano	Chicken with Ginger and honey 9
	Ginger and honey glazed ham 93		Warm winter salad with honey and vegetables 44
	Glamorgan sausage 35		
	Honey chicken and noodle stir-fry 15	Paprika	Pork spare ribs with honey and garlic 10
	Honey roast squash with vegetable couscous 38	Parsley	Glamorgan sausage 35
	Honey roasted vegetable couscous 37		Honey glazed carrots and shallots 96
	Honeyed lamb and vegetable stir-fry 14		Honey roast squash with vegetables and couscous 38
	Lamb shanks with honey 12		Mackerel with honey and herb stuffing 28
	Pork spare ribs with honey and garlic 10		St David's Day chicken with honeyed leeks 21
	Spiced red cabbage with honey 95		Winter salad with turkey and a honey and mustard vinaigrette 43
	Summer salad with feta cheese and honey dressing 41		

Parsnips	Honey seeded roots 97 Parsnips with a mustard and honey glaze 94	Raisins	Summer salad with feta cheese and honey dressing 41
		Red Cabbage	Spiced red cabbage with honey 95
Peaches	Honey cheesecake with fresh peaches 52		
		Red Wine	Cranberry honey and ginger sauce 93
Pears	Autumn crumble with honey and chocolate 55 Pear tart with honey and marzipan 49		Lamb shanks with honey 12
		Rhubarb	Rhubarb tart with orange and honey 56
Pepper (Veg)	Honey chicken and noodle stir-fry 15	Rice Krispies	Chocolate honey Krispies 87
	Honey roast squash with vegetables and couscous 38	Rocket	Autumn salad with chicken and a spicy pumpkin and honey
	Honey roasted vegetable couscous 37		dressing 42
	Honeyed lamb and vegetable stir-fry 14	Rolled Oats	Autumn crumble with honey and chocolate 55
	Oriental honeyed pork or chicken 20		Country nut biscuits 82
	Sauce for salmon 32		Honey fruit fingers 101
	Winter salad with turkey and a honey and mustard vinaigrette 43		Honey oat chocolate flapjacks 86 Muesli bars with honey 84 Oat and sultana honey
Pineapple	Oriental honeyed pork or chicken 20		biscuits 84
		Rosemary	Chicken thighs with lemon honey and potato wedges 13
Plums	Autumn crumble with honey and chocolate 55		Lamb shanks with honey 12
Pork	Oriental honeyed pork or chicken 20	Rum	Special honey Christmas cake 92
	Pork spare ribs with honey and garlic 10	Salad beans	Autumn salad with chicken and a spicy pumpkin and honey
	Roast loin of pork with special honey apple sauce 11		dressing 42
Potatoes	Chicken thighs with lemon honey and potato wedges 13	Salad leaves	Spring salad with honey and caramelised walnuts 40
	Winter salad with turkey and a honey and mustard vinaigrette 43		Winter salad with turkey and a honey and mustard vinaigrette 43
Prunes	A special refrigerator cake 79	Salmon	Salmon fillet baked with lemon and honey 26
Radish	Spring salad with honey and caramelised walnuts 40		Salmon steaks with dill and honey sauce 31
Raisins	Chocolate honey Krispies 87 Glamorgan honey fruit cake 77 Snowdon Pudding 46 Special honey Christmas cake 92	Sausage	Sausages with mustard and honey 9 Sticky honey sausages 94

Sea Bass	Baked sea bass with honey and lemongrass 24	Spinach	Warm winter salad with honey and vegetables 44 Winter salad with turkey and a honey and mustard vinaigrette 43
Seeds	Autumn salad with chicken and a spicy honey dressing 42 Muesli bars with honey 84 Summer salad with feta cheese and honey dressing 41	Spring onions	Cod with coconut and honey 25 Ginger and turkey meatballs with honey sauce 16 Honey and mandarin swordfish 29 Sauce for salmon 32 Spicy beef medallions with sesame honey 6
Sesame Seeds	Honey chicken and noodle stir-fry 15 Honey seeded roots 97 Sauce for salmon 32 Soy honey chicken with sesame seeds 7 Spicy beef medallions with sesame honey 6	Star Anise	Mulled cider with honey 102
Shallots	Honey glazed carrots and shallots 96 Winter salad with turkey and a honey and mustard vinaigrette 43	Stem Ginger	A special honey refrigerator cake 79 Honey and spice cake with lemon and ginger topping 76 Special honey Christmas cake 92
Sherry	Chicken with honey lemon sauce 19	Strawberries	Strawberry honey mousse 60
Single Cream	Leek terrine with honey and mustard vinaigrette 39	Suet	Snowdon pudding 46
Soy Sauce	Chicken marinated in honey and mead 18 Chicken with ginger and honey 9 Chicken with honey lemon sauce 19 Ginger and turkey meatballs with honey sauce 16 Haddock with honey soy dressing 30 Honey and mandarin swordfish 29 Honey chicken and noodle stir-fry 15 Honeyed lamb and vegetable stir-fry 14 Oriental honeyed pork or chicken 20 Soy honey chicken with sesame spinach 7 Spicy beef medallions with sesame honey 6	Sultanas	Apple and honey pudding 53 Baked apple with honey and Amaretti stuffing 50 Bara brith 73 Bread and butter pudding 48 Family apple cake 67 Glamorgan honey fruit cake 77 Honey and apple slab cake 69 Honey carrot cake 71 Honey oat chocolate flapjacks 86 Honey Welsh cakes 78 Muesli bars with honey 84 Oat and Sultana honey biscuits 84 Special honey Christmas cake 92 Teisen Lap with honey 66
		Swede	Honey seeded roots 97 Warm Winter salad with honey and vegetables 44
Spinach	Soy honey chicken with sesame spinach 7	Sweet Corn	Honey chicken and noodle stir-fry 15 Honey roast corn on the cob 36

111

Sweet Corn	Honeyed lamb and vegetable stir-fry 14	White wine	Leek terrine with honey and mustard vinaigrette 39 Orange and lemon carrots with honey 96
Swordfish	Honey and mandarin swordfish 29		
		Worcester Sauce	Lamb shanks with honey 12
Tarragon	Mackerel with honey and herb stuffing 28		
Thyme	Chicken thighs with lemon honey and potato wedges 13 Ginger and honey glazed ham 93 Ginger and turkey meatballs with honey sauce 16 Spiced red cabbage with honey 95 Welsh lamb with orange and honey 8		
Tomatoes	Oriental honeyed pork or chicken 20 Sauce for salmon 32 Summer salad with feta cheese and honey dressing 41 Winter salad with turkey and honey and mustard vinaigrette 43		
Turkey	Ginger and turkey meatballs with honey sauce 16 Winter salad with turkey and a honey and mustard vinaigrette 43		
Turmeric	Cod with coconut and honey 25		
Vanilla Extract	Bread and butter 48 Chocolate and honey pecan tart 47 Chocolate chip 90 Family apple cake 67 Honey cranberry biscotti 100 Special honey Christmas cake 92		
Vanilla Pod	Honey ice cream 61 Mulled cider with honey 102		
Watercress	Autumn salad with chicken and a spicy pumpkin and honey dressing 42		
Whiskey	Chocolate honey mousse 59		

www.ingramcontent.com/pod-product-compliance
Lightning Source LLC
Chambersburg PA
CBHW050816090426
42736CB00021B/3472